I dedicate this book to my three children, Tyler, Ian, and Moriah. You have been my motivation and inspiration for the research and program development, and, ultimately, for my putting these thoughts to paper. Watching you navigate traditional school structures that I helped design created in me a sense of urgency that I could not ignore. We can do better. You deserved better. I love you.

**—Timothy Stuart**

I dedicate this book to my parents, Karin and Peter Heckmann. You have given me the courage to take risks, the passion to chase my dreams, and the belief that I can change the world. You gave me the gift of agency and I only hope this book extends that gift to many others!

**—Sascha Heckmann**

I dedicate this book to my dear friend Rebecca DuFour. Your wisdom and support have profoundly impacted my work, the PLC at Work process, and education across the world. I look forward to advancing the PLC message and Rick's legacy together for years to come.

**—Mike Mattos**

I dedicate this book to the love of my life, Lesley Anne Buffum.

**—Austin Buffum**

D1473236

# Personalized LEARNING

in a PLC at Work™

Student Agency Through the
Four Critical Questions

Timothy S. **STUART**
Sascha **HECKMANN**
Mike **MATTOS**
Austin **BUFFUM**

Solution Tree | Press

*a division of*
Solution Tree

555 North Morton Street
Bloomington, IN 47404
800.733.6786 (toll free) / 812.336.7700
FAX: 812.336.7790

email: info@SolutionTree.com
SolutionTree.com

Visit **go.SolutionTree.com/PLCbooks** to download the free reproducibles in this book.

Printed in the United States of America

22   21   20   19   18                1   2   3   4   5

Library of Congress Cataloging-in-Publication Data

Names: Stuart, Timothy S., author.

Title: Personalized learning in a PLC at Work : student agency through the four critical questions Timothy S. Stuart, Sascha Heckmann, Mike Mattos, and Austin Buffum.

Description: Bloomington, IN : Solution Tree Press, 2018. | Includes bibliographical references and index.

Identifiers: LCCN 2017049822 | ISBN 9781942496595 (perfect bound)

Subjects: LCSH: Professional learning communities. | Individualized instruction. | Motivation in education. | Educational change. | Response to intervention (Learning disabled children)

Classification: LCC LB1731 .S747 2018 | DDC 371.102--dc23 LC record available at https://lccn.loc.gov/2017049822

**Solution Tree**

Jeffrey C. Jones, CEO
Edmund M. Ackerman, President

**Solution Tree Press**

*President and Publisher:* Douglas M. Rife
*Editorial Director:* Sarah Payne-Mills
*Art Director:* Rian Anderson
*Managing Production Editor:* Kendra Slayton
*Senior Production Editor:* Suzanne Kraszewski
*Senior Editor:* Amy Rubenstein
*Copy Editor:* Ashante K. Thomas
*Proofreader:* Jessi Finn
*Cover Designer:* Rian Anderson

# Acknowledgments

Many people have contributed to our thinking and rethinking about this work since its conception. We express our gratitude and appreciation to those who have inspired us to give this project a go, encouraged us when we encountered challenges in the process, and reminded us of the value of this book's important message. Thanks to all of you who have served as sounding boards, guinea pigs, and guardrails.

Rick and Becky DuFour and Bob Eaker, your inspiration, guidance, and encouragement throughout our professional learning community (PLC) journey have been life changing for all of us. We are deeply indebted to you. PLC has so profoundly impacted teachers and students around the world. Thank you for encouraging us to explore how to bring students into the collective responsibility for learning. Our hope is that this book will serve to inspire educators to thoughtfully (and sometimes wildly) give students agency over their own learning so that they can learn at an even higher level.

A huge thank-you to all the educators who have contributed their stories to this book. Your impact goes far beyond these chapters. Ollie Baker, Daniel Birch, Simon Bright, Cris Ewell, Dan Kerr, Laura Jo Evans, Saba Ghole, Bob Helmer, Sarah Martin, Darlene Poluan, David Redmond, Dennis Steigerwald, Kyle Wagner, Katie Walthall, and Fiona Zinn, your programs and schools have served as models to us, and your work has helped us believe that the theory of personalized learning can be put into practice. We hope your stories will serve to inspire thousands more educators to begin the process of returning agency for learning back to students. We trust that this book honors your work, your hearts, and your commitment to personalized learning. Thanks for being vulnerable and courageous enough to share your stories.

To the entire Singapore American School leadership team and faculty, we thank you for planting a flag so bravely on the summit of personalized learning in a context of unwavering excellence and climbing toward it, step by step. In many ways, your *why* is our *why*, your journey is our journey, your lessons are our lessons, and your change process serves as an inspiration for schools around the world. Thank you.

Mona, once again your fingerprints are all over this book. Your keen editorial eye, sharp mind, and gift of turning complex rambling into a sharp message have made this a better book. Thanks for the hours of selfless editing you committed to this project. To our families for their relentless support and inspiration—without you, none of this would be possible.

Nola, thank you for being a thought partner, for contributing your unique perspectives as an innovative educator, and for spending hours talking through the most complex ideas in the book to make them comprehensible and impactful.

Finally, we would like to thank all students and teachers who are challenging and changing the global educational paradigm every day. You are the ones who know how hard it is to change an embedded narrative, but you do it with intention, courage, and hope. This book is about you and for you.

Solution Tree Press would like to thank the following reviewers:

Lynmara Colón
Principal
Mary Williams Elementary School
Dumfries, Virginia

Samantha Hurst
Fourth-Grade Teacher
Borden Elementary School
Borden, Indiana

Heather Silvia
Principal
Donlin Drive Elementary School
Liverpool, New York

Timothy M. Wagner
Associate High School Principal for
    Program Planning and Innovation
Upper St. Clair High School
Upper St. Clair, Pennsylvania

Stacy Winslow
Assistant to the Superintendent for
    Curriculum, Instruction, and
    Assessment
Derry Township School District
Hershey, Pennsylvania

Visit **go.SolutionTree.com/PLCbooks** to download the free reproducibles in this book.

# Table of Contents

# About the Authors

 **Timothy S. Stuart, EdD,** is the head of school at the International Community School of Addis Ababa. Previously, Tim served as the executive director of strategic programs at the Singapore American School. In this role, Tim served as the chief architect for research and development and supported strategic school reform. He is the former high school principal of Singapore American School, where he led his division through the professional learning community (PLC) implementation process, culminating in its recognition as a PLC exemplar school. Tim also served as the high school principal of Jakarta Intercultural School (JIS), where he helped introduce PLCs. JIS is now also recognized as a PLC exemplar school. Tim has been an international and cross-cultural educator for twenty-seven years, serving schools in the United States, Turkey, Switzerland, Indonesia, Singapore, and Ethiopia.

Tim is the editor of *Global Perspectives: Professional Learning Communities at Work™ in International Schools* as well as a contributing author. He is a contributing author to *It's About Time: Planning Interventions and Extensions in Secondary School.* He is the coauthor of *Children at Promise: 9 Principles to Help Kids Thrive in an At-Risk World* and *Raising Children at Promise: How the Surprising Gifts of Adversity and Relationship Build Character in Kids.* Tim's research and writing reflect his passion for creating optimal school environments so that all students can learn at high levels.

Tim is the cofounder of 8 Degrees Up, an educational consulting firm that specializes in supporting schools in making the shift to personalized learning through student empowerment and agency.

Tim holds a doctor of education from Seattle Pacific University, a master's degree from The College of New Jersey, and a bachelor of arts degree from Wheaton College.

To learn more about Tim's work, follow @drtstuart on Twitter.

**Sascha Heckmann, EdD,** is an innovative practitioner with broad experience in a variety of contexts. He is currently director at the American International School of Mozambique. Previously, he was the high school principal at Shanghai American School, where he leveraged the Professional Learning Communities at Work (PLC) model as the foundation for innovative and progressive teaching and learning. During his time in Shanghai, Sascha created the Innovation Institute, a transdisciplinary, project-based learning community that empowers students to personalize their learning through agency. Sascha has worked in a wide variety of schools ranging from private schools, international schools, U.S. public schools, and alternative school settings.

Sascha is the founder of 8 Degrees Up, an educational consulting firm that specializes in supporting schools in making the shift to personalized learning through student empowerment and agency.

Sascha holds a doctorate of education in organizational leadership from the University of La Verne and a master's degree in education from California State University, Bakersfield.

To learn more about Sascha's work, visit www.8degreesup.com, or follow @8degreesup on Twitter.

**Mike Mattos** is an internationally recognized author, presenter, and practitioner who specializes in uniting teachers, administrators, and support staff to transform schools by implementing the response to intervention (RTI) and PLC processes. Mike co-created the RTI at Work model, which builds on the foundation of the PLC at Work process by using team structures and a focus on learning, collaboration, and results to drive successful outcomes and creating systematic, multitiered systems of supports to ensure high levels of learning for all students.

He is former principal of Marjorie Veeh Elementary School and Pioneer Middle School in California. At both schools, Mike helped create powerful PLCs, improving learning for all students. In 2004, Marjorie Veeh, an elementary school with a large population of youth at risk, won the California Distinguished School and National Title I Achieving School awards.

A National Blue Ribbon School, Pioneer is among only thirteen schools in the United States that the GE Foundation selected as a Best-Practice Partner and is one of eight schools that Richard DuFour chose to feature in the video series *The Power of Professional Learning Communities at Work: Bringing the Big Ideas to Life*. Based on standardized test scores, Pioneer ranks among the top 1 percent of California secondary schools and, in 2009 and 2011, was named Orange County's top middle school. For his leadership, Mike was named the Orange County Middle School Administrator of the Year by the Association of California School Administrators.

Mike has coauthored many other books focused on RTI and PLCs, including *Learning by Doing: A Handbook for Professional Learning Communities at Work (3rd edition)*; *Concise Answers to Frequently Asked Questions About Professional Learning Communities at Work*; *Simplifying Response to Intervention: Four Essential Guiding Principles*; *Pyramid Response to Intervention: RTI, Professional Learning Communities, and How to Respond When Kids Don't Learn*; *Uniting Academic and Behavior Interventions: Solving the Skill or Will Dilemma*; *It's About Time: Planning Interventions and Extensions in Secondary School*; *It's About Time: Planning Interventions and Extensions in Elementary School*; *Best Practices at Tier 1: Daily Differentiation for Effective Instruction, Secondary*; *Best Practices at Tier 1: Daily Differentiation for Effective Instruction, Elementary*; *The Collaborative Administrator: Working Together as a Professional Learning Community*; and *Taking Action: A Handbook for RTI at Work*.

To learn more about Mike's work, visit AllThingsPLC (www.allthingsplc.info) and http://mattos.info, or follow @mikemattos65 on Twitter.

**Austin Buffum, EdD,** has forty-seven years of experience in public schools. His many roles include serving as former senior deputy superintendent of California's Capistrano Unified School District. Austin has presented in over nine hundred school districts throughout the United States and around the world. He delivers trainings and presentations on the RTI at Work model. This tiered approach to response to intervention is centered on PLC at Work concepts and strategies to ensure every student receives the time and support necessary to succeed. Austin also delivers workshops and presentations that provide the tools educators need to build and sustain PLCs.

Austin was selected as the 2006 Curriculum and Instruction Administrator of the Year by the Association of California School Administrators. He attended the Principals' Center at the Harvard Graduate School of Education and was greatly inspired by its founder, Roland Barth, an early advocate of the collaborative culture that defines PLCs today. He later led Capistrano's K–12 instructional program on an increasingly collaborative path toward operating as a PLC. During this process, thirty-seven of the district's schools were designated California Distinguished Schools, and eleven received National Blue Ribbon recognition.

Austin is coauthor with Suzette Lovely of *Generations at School: Building an Age-Friendly Learning Community.* He has also coauthored *Uniting Academic and Behavior Interventions: Solving the Skill or Will Dilemma; It's About Time: Planning Interventions and Extensions in Elementary School; It's About Time: Planning Interventions and Extensions in Secondary School; Simplifying Response to Intervention: Four Essential Guiding Principles; Pyramid Response to Intervention: RTI, Professional Learning Communities, and How to Respond When Kids Don't Learn;* and *Taking Action: A Handbook for RTI at Work.*

A graduate of the University of Southern California, Austin earned a bachelor of music degree and received a master of education degree with honors. He holds a doctor of education degree from Nova Southeastern University.

To learn more about Austin's work, follow @agbuffum on Twitter.

To book Timothy S. Stuart, Sascha Heckmann, Mike Mattos, or Austin Buffum for professional development, contact pd@SolutionTree.com.

# Introduction

It seems as if every other day there is a new innovative school featured in the news. Each time the report showcases unique or even daring learning environments, stunning learning results, highly engaged learners, and inspired educators. The more we hear about these schools, the more we wonder, "What makes them so noteworthy? Are they really successful? Do they have a secret sauce that we should try? Or, are they just one-off wonders due to their unique locations or the type of students they serve? Could it even be that the whole trend toward innovation is smoke and mirrors or another fad—the illusion of newfound relevance and success without any sound or reliable substance that can ultimately last?"

Between August 2014 and December 2017, we visited hundreds of schools in our collective experience as speakers, leaders, and learners. More than one hundred of these visits were to the most forward-thinking, progressive, and innovative schools across four continents. The goal? To come to a deeper understanding of what high-performing schools have in common, what is truly working, and what is not. Our travels have taken us to public and charter schools, independent and international schools, schools serving affluent communities, and schools serving some of the poorest communities in the world. One of the most evident and humbling observations we made was that teachers and schools around the world earnestly want what is best for the students they serve. Teachers from every corner of the globe care for their students and want to do everything in their power to equip them, at a minimum, to live happy, fulfilling lives of positive contribution to society.

As we were visiting these schools, we realized there is no secret for successful innovation. In fact, some of the schools, while very innovative, did not produce high levels of learning. However, the schools that stood out had some clear commonalities. Those commonalities weren't exorbitant funding, or world-class facilities, or a distinct caliber of student. It became clear that the most successful schools had deliberate systems and structures to ensure that each student attained high levels of learning. We identified three clear elements that are common among the schools that are both progressive in design and excellent in outcome.

1. These schools have all the characteristics of high-functioning PLCs, even if they do not use that nomenclature.

2. They focus on essential disciplinary knowledge; incorporate transdisciplinary, future-ready skills; and cultivate student-agency behaviors.

3. They teach students how to personalize their learning process.

The highly effective and learning-progressive schools we observed had a well-articulated guaranteed and viable curriculum composed of both critical disciplinary and transdisciplinary skills. The teachers took collective responsibility for student learning, actively collaborated, used laser-focused learning outcomes, established common expectations for learning, and provided timely feedback. They also acted on the information from formative assessments to differentiate learning through intervention and acceleration strategies. In other words, knowingly or unknowingly, the most successful forward-thinking schools used PLC strategies with response to intervention (RTI) constructs (or recognizable facsimiles) as their core framework for innovation.

Finally, these schools developed mutual partnerships with students in the learning process. They cultivated intrinsic motivation, something that empowered students to own their learning. The most successful highly effective and learning-progressive schools honored their students' unique attributes, developed positive relationships focused on students' strengths and passions, provided personalized learning structures, and empowered students to drive their learning. To a large degree, the students had a voice in what they learned, in plotting their plans toward learning outcomes, and in deciding how to demonstrate their proficiency. While teachers and students had different roles, the students in the most effective learning-progressive schools were equal partners in the learning journey. Importantly, these schools did not mistake student empowerment as a way to diminish the faculty's responsibility in ensuring every student's success. Instead, the staff's collaborative efforts and systems of intervention provided the supports—and safety nets—students need to take risks, make mistakes, and ultimately succeed. It is evident that these schools took their commitment to creating lifelong learners very seriously.

As we reflected on these commonalities, we began to wonder how we could translate these attributes to action steps to help more schools. What is the difference between PLC schools that attain great success in the guaranteed and viable curriculum and the highly effective and learning-progressive schools we observed? The difference, we concluded, is the active involvement and partnership of the students in the PLC process. To go from being highly effective to being highly effective and transformative requires more than teachers strategizing about student learning through the PLC process; students need to be engaged in the PLC process themselves. Students must own their learning by asking and answering for themselves the four critical questions of a PLC (DuFour, DuFour, Eaker, Many, & Mattos, 2016). Table I.1 shows the application of the four critical questions to students.

TABLE I.1: The Four Critical Questions of a PLC for Students

| Four Critical Questions of a PLC | Modification for Students |
|---|---|
| 1. What do we want all students to know and be able to do? | 1. What do I want to know, understand, and be able to do? |
| 2. How will we know if they learn it? | 2. How will I demonstrate that I have learned it? |
| 3. How will we respond when some students do not learn? | 3. What will I do when I am not learning? |
| 4. How will we extend the learning for students who are already proficient? | 4. What will I do when I have already learned it? |

## About This Book

This book presents a clear and concise case for transforming the current educational paradigm in order to future-proof students. We demonstrate how PLC schools can take the next step in the journey: to become highly effective and learning-progressive (innovative) PLC schools in which students experience student agency, mastering the guaranteed and viable curriculum while personalizing their learning and cultivating the skills and dispositions to become future-ready, lifelong learners.

If your school is just exploring the impact that PLCs can have on student learning, this book will give you a brief yet thorough overview of PLCs and their undeniable impact. If your school is already a PLC and you are wondering whether the PLC construct has relevance for the 21st century learner, this book will affirm that you are on the right path and give you concrete strategies about how to use this research-based and time-tested approach to help reach even higher levels of engagement and learning for all students.

This book is divided into four parts. Part I, "Making the Case for Change," chapters 1, 2, and 3, describes the changing educational paradigm, defines what it means to be highly effective and learning progressive, and introduces the elements of these innovative schools. We then explore the concepts of personalized learning and student agency through the PLC framework in part II, "Adapting the Four Critical Questions." Chapters 4, 5, and 6 give a structure for a thoughtful release of each PLC critical question for students based on desired learning outcomes. In part III, "Putting Theory Into Practice," chapters 7, 8, and 9 give examples of how elementary, middle, and high schools around the world are putting theory into practice. In part IV, "Committing to Change," chapter 10 introduces a successful change process in a highly respected school that has gone through the transformation to the next level of learning as a highly effective and learning-progressive school.

## Inquiry and Reflection

Since we are theorists and practitioners who believe in the power of collective inquiry, we want to help you begin your own inquiry process. At the end of many chapters, we include a synthesis of key insights—Tips for Transformation—that allow you to personalize your own learning pathway. In the Rate Your Progression sections, you will measure your progress or your school's progress toward becoming a highly effective and learning-progressive school. These features offer some additional structure and provocation for your learning journey. We also feature Questions to Consider in each chapter for further reflection. These questions are conversation starters for your collaborative teams within your PLC. If you are reading the book independently, we recommend that you process your answers to these questions with a trusted colleague in your school or school district, starting a dialogue that will lead you forward.

We have structured these Questions to Consider around the four critical questions of a PLC. They focus on four main areas.

1.  **The learning:** What are the important learnings for me in this chapter? For my school? What am I inspired to know and be able to do?

2.  **The evidence:** What are we already doing that aligns with this paradigm? What would change in my school and professional experience if we further embrace and implement it?

3.  **The learning pit:** What obstacles would we face if we were to try or to further this approach? What strategies could we use to experience breakthroughs?

4.  **The lever:** What would we need to accelerate the change process?

These are great questions for students to ask as part of their learning process, so we encourage you to apply them in your instructional work with students.

Our hope is that this book will be a useful tool for all PLC schools that are ready to deepen their understanding and implementation of PLCs by welcoming students into the PLC conversation and empowering them to truly own and personalize their learning. Additionally, this book serves as a useful guide for learning-progressive schools aspiring to become highly effective, ensuring that all students learn at high levels with measurable results. We hope this book will serve as a resource that you can go back to regardless of where your school finds itself on the journey. If you are wondering where you are on the journey, begin by asking yourself critical question 1: "What is it that you really want your students to know and be able to do?" Then, ask yourself if your school provides the learning experiences necessary for your students to learn that and obtain the skills necessary to be successful participants in, and active contributors to, this ever-changing world.

# PART ONE

# Making the Case for Change

# 1

# A Changing
# Educational Paradigm

One innovative school we visited is a highly successful secondary school in Finland—and not just any school. We visited one of the highest-ranked schools in what some consider the highest-ranked country for education. This school challenged almost everything we thought to be standard for high schools. We saw students designing almost entirely their own path to graduation—both the actual path and the courses they took along the path. One student commented that it didn't matter how many years a student took to finish high school. He said, "If it takes you three years, that's fine; if it takes you five years, that's fine as well." Wow, we thought, a school that truly put into practice the notion that learning is the constant and time is the variable.

All too often, we expect the highest-performing schools to settle into the status quo as they polish their excellence. Indeed, schools built successfully with traditional methods can find it difficult to harness the institutional will to change once complacency sets in. However, this is not the case at this Finnish school.

Educators there push forward with a stunning sense of urgency. We asked the principal about the school's remarkable motivation. How has the staff stayed so focused to move from a traditional to a highly effective and learning-progressive model when, educationally, the school is already considered number one in the country? The principal's answer was interesting: "Every day my teachers and I must drive past the Nokia offices down the street from our school to get to work. It serves as a strong reminder of what will happen to our school if we don't change: how and what our students learn will become like Nokia, irrelevant in the 21st century." You see, Nokia was one of the leading phone companies in the world until the introduction of the iPhone by Apple in 2007. Almost overnight, Apple's stocks soared and Nokia stocks tanked.

In 2013, Microsoft purchased Nokia. In an article about the acquisition, Ziyad Jawabra (2016) explains:

> Nokia has been a respectable company. They didn't do anything wrong in their business, however, the world changed too fast. Their opponents were too powerful. They missed out on learning, they missed out on changing, and thus they lost the opportunity at hand to make it big. Not only did they miss the opportunity to earn big money, they lost their chance of survival.

Much like with Nokia, our students' needs are changing and many modern-day schools are not keeping up with the change.

In this chapter, we begin by exploring the foundation of our modern-day schools. We contrast this foundation with the skills students will need in the workplace of the future and how they master these skills with future-ready learning within a global, progressive educational landscape. We define what it means to be a highly effective and learning-progressive school and how schools achieve this status through personalized learning.

## Preparation for the Past

The foundations of our modern-day schools are deeply rooted in the development of an industrial economy (Urban & Wagoner, 2013). The purpose of school in its original conception was to train young people in a systematic, uniform manner to acquire specific content knowledge and prescribed skills for a lifelong career. Globally, education systems, including those in the United States, were designed to engage students in a standardized experience that prepared them to play a specific role in society. Schools separated and groomed a limited number of students who excelled in the standard experience for postsecondary education and professional careers. Schools trained students who did not perform as well in the general curriculum to be contributors to society through the acquisition of specific skills that held value in the economy. Universal access to education was based in the industrial economy, and its legacy is prevalent in virtually every aspect of contemporary schools.

The school of the past, what is familiar to many teachers and parents, was based on several core ideals (Wayne & Wagoner, 2013). First, the teacher was the knower and the student was the learner. In the industrial model, the teacher held discrete knowledge to transmit to students. The student's role was to be attentive and retain the knowledge he or she received from the expert teacher. The teacher expected students to model behaviors that made them open and receptive. Second, schools existed to sort students into discrete economic castes. The students that schools deemed more capable were able to receive and retain more information, and schools designated those students as smart or gifted. They gained access to a university education and ultimately white-collar careers. The students that schools deemed weaker were sorted into a less-academically-rigorous, hands-on, experience-focused, blue-collar-career-readiness track. Finally, schools provided a uniform experience: students took the same subjects and learned the same content, and schools measured them on the same criteria. The construct of equal being fair was a hallmark of the industrial education.

This model of education is strongly imprinted on contemporary education as seen in honors programs; remedial education; percentage grades; the bell curve; the teacher as expert, student as novice model; the layout of classrooms that students and staff access from a central hallway; transcripts; Carnegie Units; content standards; standardized tests—the list goes on. To move beyond this traditional model, we must acknowledge it as our foundation and also honor it as appropriate for its time and era. We must also recognize the need to evolve from the traditional model as our economy has transitioned into a post-industrial period. If we are to adequately prepare students for an uncertain future economy, our focus as educators must be on rapidly shifting to a learning-progressive model of education. The future for learning-progressive education is bright. As philosopher Eric Hoffer (2006) indicates, "In times of drastic change it is the learner that inherits the future. The learned usually find themselves equipped to live in a world that no longer exists" (p. 32). Learning-progressive schools are able to shift focus from producing learned graduates, to producing graduates that are skilled learners. They don't prepare students for the past and do focus on producing students that are future-ready, lifelong learners.

## The Workplace of the Future

We are living during the most rapidly changing period in history. The rise of technology has fundamentally changed the way we experience the world. Technological innovations have dramatically shifted the way we live and, as a result, the knowledge and skills we will need in the future to fully participate in society. The demands on schools have changed as well. School was historically a moderate guarantee for a prosperous future as the world was stable. The expectation has been this: do well in school, go to a good university, and the world will be available to you. But in the 21st century global economy, this road is far less certain. If educators are earnest about equipping students for a new reality, we must honestly examine what demands the future will place on our graduates.

Predicting the future of education is challenging, yet several prominent research organizations dedicate significant resources to helping inform educators about what lies ahead. What is clear from their collective studies is that, in the future, knowledge will no longer be the primary currency of success. Increasingly, the value of knowledge comes from what you are able to do with it. In its study *The Future of Work*, the Institute for the Future (IFTF, 2007) identifies trends that impact the workplace. Table 1.1 summarizes these workplace trends that have become the reality for students in our schools (IFTF, 2007).

TABLE 1.1: Future Workplace Trends and Their Impact on the Workplace

| Trend | Impact on the Workplace |
|---|---|
| **The Amplified Individual** | The workplace of the future will shift from a focus on the individual to a focus on the collective where work is social, interactive, and improvisational and where technology augments it. |
| **The Visible World** | The workplace is full with data and information that will change the way we find, create, and communicate knowledge. |
| **Diversity Redefined** | The innovative workplace will reimage the construct of diversity from gender and race to new dimensions including age, skills, thinking styles, and many others. |
| **Science at Work** | The workplace will focus on human-centered design that uses biology and neurosciences to change the work ecosystem to inspire creativity, boost innovation, and improve employees' quality of life. |
| **Sustainable Enterprise** | The workplace of the future will make sustainability part of the core business as ethical impact becomes the driver for individual and corporate decisions. |
| **Health in the Workplace** | More and more employees will value their long-term health, thus shifting employers' focus to improving workplace conditions. |

*Source: Adapted from IFTF, 2007.*

This study makes a clear statement that the workplace demands different skills and dispositions from those valued in the industrial age. The challenge for schools is to create a curriculum, a learning environment, and systems of support that will cultivate these skills and dispositions in students.

# Future-Ready Learning

Schools and the educators within them are well intentioned; they want to believe the education they provide is good for students. They want to produce graduates who will thrive. Unfortunately, we believe many schools fall into the trap of preparing students for the past rather than focusing on learning that will prepare students for the future. The world has evolved rapidly while education slowly evolves, creating an ever-increasing relevance gap for students.

What schools must do is look intentionally at research and provide a more authentic learning environment that is workplace and life relevant. Highly effective *and* learning-progressive schools have evolved to meet their students' learning needs, to equip students to internalize the skills and behaviors necessary to be true lifelong learners. One of the greatest challenges in becoming a highly effective and learning-progressive school is balancing knowledge and skills learning outcomes. All educators would agree that some amount of knowledge is absolutely necessary to be an educated person, but how much is enough? In his book *Future Wise*, Harvard professor David N. Perkins (2014) wrestles with the long-argued question of what is worth knowing to produce future-ready graduates. Perkins (2014) suggests we ask ourselves a simple question to determine what is worth knowing: "Is what a student is learning likely to matter in the life of the learner and to his or her future?" The question is intentionally broad and contextual as to not limit the possible outcomes. In its openness comes its beauty; for learning to be meaningful, it must be relevant and useful for learners—not for their teachers.

Perkins (2014) also notes that what we teach in traditional schools may not be what's best to prepare students to be ideal citizens, workers, or community members in the future. He argues that schools must get beyond the traditional framework of schooling to better prepare students for the future. He identifies what he refers to as the *six beyond* that support schools in producing future-ready learners (Perkins, 2014).

1. **Beyond basic skills:** Schools have to empower students with 21st century skills and dispositions that go beyond the traditional skills of reading, writing, and arithmetic.

2. **Beyond traditional disciplines:** Educators must embrace new disciplines that are hybrid and less familiar and morph key ideas for different disciplines.

3. **Beyond discrete disciplines:** Modern curricula must engage students in contemporary, relevant problems that transcend the boundaries of disciplines and are interdisciplinary in nature.

4. **Beyond regional perspectives:** Schools must take a global view and incorporate issues of global significance that require multiple perspectives to develop global citizenship.

5. **Beyond mastering content:** Schools must demand that students use content to make connections, solve complex problems, and prompt action.

6. **Beyond prescribed content:** Educators must empower students with choice of what to learn within the core disciplines where educators work as learning coaches, not teachers.

Perkins's (2014) six beyond are one example of what is clear in a growing body of research: education must change at its core if schools are to produce future-ready students. Highly effective and learning-progressive schools embrace the challenge of incorporating knowledge, skills, and dispositions into their core program.

To gain perspective on what highly effective and learning-progressive schools do to make learning future-ready for students, we, the authors of this book, visited more than one hundred schools from around the world identified as highly innovative or progressive.

# The Global, Progressive Education Landscape

The diverse collection of public, charter, independent, international, and foreign public schools we visited included unified early learning to grade 12 systems; independent elementary, middle, and high schools; and networks of schools. Each school or school system has its own version of progressive education and comprises dedicated teachers committed to their students and working tirelessly to produce future-ready learners. Unilaterally, these schools display a compelling vision and intentional actions. Every school we visited aspires to be innovative, its mission statements including such phrases as *lifelong learner*, *global citizen*, *educational excellence*, and some version of *success after graduation*. In addition to such basic commonalities, we found some interesting patterns in the global education landscape with three types of schools: (1) highly effective schools, (2) learning-progressive schools, and (3) highly effective *and* learning-progressive schools.

## Highly Effective Schools

Highly effective schools are schools that receive accolades for their achievement under traditional measures of success. They have what Robert Marzano (2003a) refers to as a guaranteed and viable curriculum for core disciplinary knowledge, and their students consistently are able to master the curriculum. In these schools, traditional education metrics are strong; however, these schools largely neglect transdisciplinary skills, the skills that transfer between and across disciplines, in their curriculum. Also, their instructional pedagogy is traditional with only small amounts of innovative programming. These schools have a lot of flash—like interesting products, innovation centers, or well-marketed innovation programs—but there is an absence of real future-focused outcomes for learners. We suggest that these schools are highly effective, but they are definitely not learning progressive. Generally, these schools offer programming that marks the construct of innovation or entrepreneurship, but the core learning is not inclusive of future-ready skills.

## Learning-Progressive Schools

Some schools we visited are amazingly innovative; the student projects and products are workplace and future relevant. The focus of these schools is almost entirely based on learner interest and learner choice. The pedagogical approaches are very innovative and learning progressive. These schools often work in nontraditional structures and outside the framework of traditional standards and assessment. Students in these schools demonstrate robust transdisciplinary skills and behaviors that lead to authentic learning experiences and regularly produce some very interesting products. However, students at these schools often have large gaps in foundational knowledge. These schools empower students with choice and relevance, but do not have a standards-based, guaranteed and viable curriculum, thus neglecting the core knowledge base students need. Students at these schools often report high levels of engagement, yet lack essential competencies to successfully access postsecondary education. We suggest that these schools are learning progressive but are not highly effective. Such a critical shortcoming can affect the perception of innovative education, drawing criticism from high-performing traditional schools and cynicism from parents who would prefer the tried-and-true to the new.

## Highly Effective *and* Learning-Progressive Schools

We discovered that schools that are both highly effective and progressive in their approach to learning are rare. These schools have highly focused disciplinary outcomes, a clearly articulated transdisciplinary skills curriculum, and a learning-progressive pedagogical approach that emphasizes specific lifelong learning outcomes. The most inspiring schools insisted on benchmarking innovation through proven results. These institutions serve as powerful exemplars for schools looking to become innovative and effective. The highly effective and learning-progressive schools we visited possess the following commonalities.

1. They embody the essential practices of PLCs.

2. They focus on essential disciplinary knowledge; incorporate transdisciplinary, future-ready skills; and cultivate student-agency behaviors.

3. They teach students how to personalize their learning process.

## Essential Practices of PLCs

Not every school we visited formally engaged in the work of the PLC process. However, every school that is highly effective and learning progressive embodies the three big ideas of a PLC (DuFour et al., 2016).

1. A focus on learning

2. A collaborative culture

3. A results orientation

Each school ensures high levels of learning for all students. Each school has specific learning outcomes, clearly articulated criteria for success, and differentiated support in the form of RTI structures to ensure students are challenged and successful. In every school, staff function as a learning community in which educators work in close collaboration. Teachers learn from each other, respect each other's unique strengths, and serve students collectively. Finally, each school focuses on results. It uses criteria-rich embedded formative assessments to actively drive learning. It implements data-collection systems, including portfolio-based assessments, that allow the school to focus on the individual success of each student to ensure all students are learning at high levels.

Another hallmark of highly effective and learning-progressive schools is that they place great emphasis on helping their students learn how to learn. Highly effective and learning-progressive schools incorporate powerful metacognitive processes to empower students to take control of their learning (discussed further in the following section). Researcher John A. C. Hattie (2008) finds that one of the greatest impacts on student learning occurs in environments where students are able to self-monitor and self-assess their learning. He states:

> The biggest effects on student learning occur when teachers become learners of their own teaching, and when students become their own teachers. When students become their own teachers they exhibit the self-regulatory attributes that seem most desirable for learners (self-monitoring, self-evaluation, self-assessment, self-teaching). (Hattie, 2008, pp. 674–681)

Hattie's (2008) emphasis on students as their own teachers is often oversimplified. He notes that both the teacher and students play vital roles in creating an environment that allows for effective partnership in the learning process. We found that highly effective and learning-progressive schools, regardless of grade level, create classrooms in which students and teachers share responsibility, and we advocate that students do this through a focus on the four critical questions of a PLC (DuFour et al., 2016), which we adapt for student use.

1. What do *I* want to know, understand, and be able to do?

2. How will *I* demonstrate that I have learned it?

3. What will *I* do when I am not learning?

4. What will *I* do when I have already learned it?

## Knowledge, Skills, and Agency

These highly effective and learning-progressive schools focus on three critical areas in instruction; they (1) focus on essential disciplinary knowledge; (2) incorporate trans-disciplinary, future-ready skills; and (3) cultivate student-agency behaviors.

### Focus on Essential Disciplinary Knowledge

The cliché "knowledge is power" is part of education pop culture and dates back to as early as the 16th century (Bartlett, 1919). In our high-tech, globally connected world, knowledge is easily accessible for anyone with an internet connection. Authors Tony Wagner and Ted Dintersmith (2016) in *Most Likely to Succeed* share that in the 21st century world, knowledge is much less valuable:

> In today's world, there is no longer a competitive advantage in knowing more than the person next to you because knowledge has become a commodity available to all with the swipe of a finger. Now, adults need to be able to ask great questions, critically analyze information, form independent opinions, collaborate, and communicate effectively. These are the skills essential for both career and citizenship. (p. 20)

With traditional knowledge readily available for students to access, highly effective and learning-progressive schools have limited the breadth of the guaranteed and viable curriculum to allow space to cultivate skills and dispositions. These schools only include content that is absolutely vital for future learning. This is not about learning less than before; it is about narrowing and deepening the content to create space for skills without compromising what students need to know to succeed in school.

Douglas Reeves (2005) identifies three criteria that allow schools to narrow the content intentionally with a clear eye on future preparation. Reeves suggests that schools use these criteria to determine which content is worthy of inclusion in a guaranteed and viable curriculum.

1. **Endurance:** Is this knowledge something the student will need for the long term?

2. **Leverage:** Will learning this content support a student's learning in other disciplines?

3. **Readiness:** Is this content an integral step in the vertical preparation of students?

This emphasis on essential learning is a critical component of highly effective and learning-progressive schools and a vehicle to intentionally narrow the content while deepening the student learning experience.

### Incorporate Transdisciplinary, Future-Ready Skills

Highly effective and learning-progressive schools place a great emphasis on the need for students to internalize transdisciplinary skills that will prepare them for their future. Transdisciplinary skills, often referred to as *21st century skills*, are those skills that have impact across disciplines and are relevant for students in life beyond school. Common agreed-on examples of these skills include critical thinking, creativity, interpersonal skills, and so forth. Highly effective and learning-progressive schools make these skills part of the guaranteed and viable curriculum.

Educators often debate which skills are the most important. The literature is filled with different schemas for organizing the skills curriculum. Table 1.2 presents a sampling of four different research-based frameworks that emphasize future-ready, transdisciplinary skills.

1. The global achievement gap (Wagner, 2008)

2. Partnership for 21st century skills (Partnership for 21st Century Learning, 2016)

3. Making thinking visible (Ritchhart, Church, & Morrison, 2011)

4. Key competences for lifelong learning (European Parliament, Council of the European Union, 2006)

**TABLE 1.2: Frameworks for 21st Century Learning**

| The Global Achievement Gap | Partnership for 21st Century Skills |
|---|---|
| Students are adept at:<br>• Thinking critically and problem solving<br>• Collaborating across networks<br>• Being agile and adaptable<br>• Showing initiative and entrepreneurship<br>• Displaying oral, written, and multimedia communication skills<br>• Accessing and analyzing information<br>• Being curious and imaginative | Students are adept at:<br>• Creativity and innovation<br>• Critical thinking and problem solving<br>• Communication<br>• Collaboration<br>• Flexibility and adaptability<br>• Initiative and self-direction<br>• Social and cross-cultural skills<br>• Productivity and accountability<br>• Leadership and responsibility<br>• Information and media literacy |

| Making Thinking Visible | Key Competences for Lifelong Learning |
|---|---|
| Students are adept at:<br><br>• Observing closely and describing what's there<br>• Building explanations and interpretations<br>• Reasoning with evidence<br>• Making connections<br>• Considering different viewpoints and perspectives<br>• Capturing the heart and forming conclusions<br>• Wondering and asking questions<br>• Uncovering complexity and going below the surface of things | Students are adept at:<br><br>• Communicating in the mother tongue<br>• Communicating in foreign languages<br>• Achieving mathematical competence and basic competences in science and technology<br>• Achieving digital competence<br>• Learning to learn<br>• Achieving social and civic competences<br>• Displaying a sense of initiative and entrepreneurship<br>• Displaying cultural awareness and expression |

Regardless of what framework they implement, highly effective and learning-progressive schools consistently select a clearly articulated set of skills that they incorporate into their guaranteed and viable curriculum.

### Cultivate Student-Agency Behaviors

Highly effective and learning-progressive schools also offer students agency in their learning to affirm the capability of students. They place deliberate emphasis on growing student agency through the cultivation of dispositions that help students succeed in school and life. *Agency* means "the capacity for an actor to act in a given environment" ("Agency (philosophy)," n.d.). Students have agency when educators allow them to be players in the educational process and when goals and visions of student learning emphasize student interests, motivations, and capabilities.

Psychologist Albert Bandura (1994) identifies the impact of what he refers to as human agency. Bandura (1994) contends that people's actions, which their self-efficacy, environmental circumstances, and specific conditions influence, have a significant impact on an outcome. Steven Hitlin and Glen H. Elder Jr. (2007) extend the work on agency and identify four distinct conceptions of agency: existential, identity, pragmatic, and life course. In this book, we focus on the latter three conceptions of agency: (1) *identity*—the beliefs we hold about ourselves and the way we want others to perceive us; (2) *pragmatic*—our ability to respond to our circumstance and effect an outcome; and (3) *life course*—believing that the actions we take will impact the future outcome. Hitlin and Elder (2007) make it clear that the final three conceptions significantly overlap and are difficult to discern in observations; thus, we define student agency as *the ability of a student to take specific and purposeful action to impact his or her level of success.*

Multiple research studies find that factors that have significant effects on student success go beyond cognition. Noncognitive factors such as student agency are becoming more important in a world that is increasingly entrepreneurial. Research studies such as *The Influence of Teaching* (Ferguson, 2015) and *Teaching Adolescents to Become Learners* (Farrington et al., 2012) demonstrate that noncognitive factors can dramatically impact student success, with student agency being one of the most important factors to success. Specifically, economist and Harvard University adjunct lecturer in public policy Ronald F. Ferguson's (2015) study *The Influence of Teaching: Beyond Standardized Test Scores—Engagement, Mindsets, and Agency* finds:

> Young people with high levels of agency do not respond passively to their circumstances; they tend to seek meaning and act with purpose to achieve the conditions they desire in their own and others' lives. The development of agency may be as important an outcome of schooling as the skills we measure with standardized testing. (p. 1)

Student agency is dependent on specific dispositions that support a student's ability to act. In this book, we use the term *dispositions* to mean the core beliefs, values, and attitudes that drive student behaviors. Specifically, we found that highly effective and learning-progressive schools focus on two primary dispositions: (1) mindset and (2) grit.

*Mindset* is a term psychologist and professor of psychology at Stanford University Carol S. Dweck (2006) popularized. In her book *Mindset: The New Psychology of Success*, Dweck identifies two mindsets—(1) fixed mindset and (2) growth mindset— and notes that every person possesses one of these two mindsets. A *fixed mindset* is the belief that one's personal qualities are final, unchanging. A person with a fixed mindset believes that he or she possesses a specific level of intelligence or type of personality. A *growth mindset* is the belief that one's personal qualities are flexible and can grow over time. A person with a growth mindset believes he or she can become more intelligent and can cultivate specific personality traits. Dweck (2006) finds that mindsets profoundly impact success in school and life. Highly effective and learning-progressive schools cultivate a growth mindset in their students.

*Grit* refers to a person's passion and perseverance. In *Grit: The Power of Passion and Perseverance*, psychologist and University of Pennsylvania professor of psychology Angela Lee Duckworth (2016) describes the dispositional quality of grit as a person's ability to consistently act on his or her passion and persevere through difficulties. Duckworth (2016) finds that grit is a strong predictor of future success and failure, especially when students face adverse circumstances. She finds that people who have the most success are frequently not the most talented, but rather are the most persistent in developing the talent they possess (Duckworth, 2016). Duckworth's (2016) findings are important to educators as she identifies grit as a dispositional quality that schools can cultivate and develop in students. We found that schools that are highly effective and learning progressive deliberately cultivate grit in their students.

## The Road to Becoming Highly Effective and Learning Progressive

Contrary to many opinions about innovation or change, we feel strongly that educators should not abandon the proven practices of past generations. Instead, we take an approach that asks schools to evolve research-based practices to best prepare students for a largely undefined and uncertain future. For schools to be relevant in the future, educators must redefine what knowledge and skills we value, and evolve the processes we engage in to cultivate the knowledge, skills, and agency behaviors of students.

We believe that the PLC process is the most powerful strategy to become a highly effective and learning-progressive school. Hattie's (2016) findings emphatically support our belief. Hattie (2016) identifies collective teacher efficacy as having one of the largest impacts on student achievement. In fact, we recommend that the effective implementation of the PLC process is foundational to becoming a highly effective and learning-progressive school.

This book provides a road map for PLC schools to focus their collaboration on learning progressive outcomes for their students. Many PLC schools have a handful of teachers who are pushing forward with innovative education. Our hope is that this book offers a construct that these educators can align with and confidently embrace. Understanding and implementing these frameworks in schools is the single most essential building block for becoming a highly effective and learning-progressive school that gives every student the opportunity to own his or her learning at high levels.

We understand that the thought of personalized learning may seem daunting. We argue it is nearly impossible in a traditional educational paradigm. Thus, we advocate for a common-sense approach where students gain the transdisciplinary skills and dispositions to own their learning. The subsequent chapters in this book share steps to becoming highly effective and learning progressive. See figure 1.1 (page 22) and the Rate Your Progression feature to see how close your school is to being both highly effective and learning progressive.

In chapter 2, we share an overview of how to incorporate student agency in the PLC process to facilitate new approaches to learning that ensure students gain the knowledge, skills, and agency behaviors that lead to personalized learning.

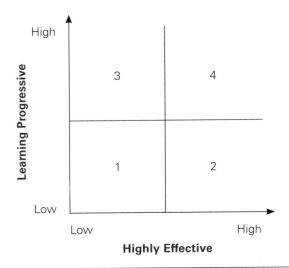

**Figure 1.1:** Highly effective and learning-progressive rating chart.

### Rate Your Progression

Considering our definition of a highly effective and learning-progressive school, in which quadrant of figure 1.1 would you place your school? What evidence do you have to support your placement?

## Tips for Transformation

The following are four tips to transform school culture.

1. **Become effective before progressive:** It is far easier to move from effective to progressive than to move from progressive to effective. Schools that have a clear curriculum and embedded collaboration tend to make the transition easier.

2. **Focus on skills and concepts:** Many schools focus far too much on content mastery as a stand-alone outcome. We found that the schools that thrive are those that use content as the vehicle to apply skills or extend learning to conceptual levels.

3. **Look to thirty:** The move to becoming a highly effective and learning-progressive school is made easier if you take the long view of success. We challenge you to think of what the indicators of success will be for your students when they are thirty years old. Too much of our conversation in schools is about immediate outcomes at age eighteen or twenty-one. Taking the long view allows us to identify what learning is "life-worthy."

4. **Shift your culture:** Empowering students with agency requires a fundamental culture shift within the school. Teachers must find their success in seeing students gain autonomy and initiative. We have to focus on how students learn, not what they learn.

## Questions to Consider

Consider the following four questions as you begin your transformation to a highly effective and learning-progressive school.

1. **The learning:** What are the important learnings for me in this chapter? For my school? What am I inspired to know and be able to do?

2. **The evidence:** What are we already doing that aligns with this paradigm? What would change in my school and professional experience if we further embrace and implement it?

3. **The learning pit:** What obstacles would we face if we were to try or to further this approach? What strategies could we use to experience breakthroughs?

4. **The lever:** What would we need to accelerate the change process?

# 2

# Student Agency for Personalized Learning

The Metropolitan Regional Career and Technical Center (The Met School) in Providence, Rhode Island, is a school dedicated to serving some of the most marginalized students in the city. When we visited this school, at first glance, it offered very few of the traditional clues that rigorous learning was actually happening. Students seemed to be very relaxed, scattered randomly throughout the campus, as if on a perpetual lunch break. This perception lasted only until we actually spoke to the students. One young woman comes to mind.

When we asked what she was working on, she said:

> Women's hips; I am studying women's hips and how they change significantly between ninth and twelfth grade. I am studying how they change and why they change from a biological perspective. I am studying how these changes impact the angles in the knees and looking at it from a physics perspective to determine how these changes in the angles impact a woman's increased chances of sports injuries and prevention strategies that should be considered. I am also doing a comprehensive literature review of women's hips throughout history and looking at how our literature and the media has portrayed women over the years, and how that portrayal has impacted the woman's psyche and what she believes about herself.

With this one self-selected and self-directed project, this student was learning more about biology, physics, geometry, history, literature, psychology, and media than most high school classes offer to the average student. This student's ability to pursue her interests and passion while demonstrating mastery of core academic competencies was most impressive.

The academic skills that students must master in a highly effective *and* learning-progressive school are extremely rigorous—far more so than the subject-specific knowledge and comprehension questions many traditional high-stakes standardized tests value. Beyond these academic skills, students must also develop complementary behaviors and dispositions, and extend their learning into areas of personal interest. And most challenging is the reality that these are the outcomes that *all* students must achieve. In our experience, many schools view these outcomes as the expectations for only their most high-achieving students; in other words, they reserve this type of rigorous curriculum for a select number of students who they deem gifted, advanced, or accelerated.

Achieving these outcomes will require educators to embrace a collaborative culture that assumes all students are worthy and capable of rigorous learning goals. They will have to adopt the most effective teaching practices to ensure every student's success. And these schools must personalize their students' learning. This doesn't mean that learning is so individualized that it lacks a pattern or structure; rather, there must be a framework in place in which students are able to take specific and purposeful action that directly impacts their level of learning (student agency). In fact, student agency is about empowering students to take control of their own learning *through organized structures* that foster high levels of learning for every student.

First, let's discuss what personalizing learning to develop student agency looks like, and then we will discuss the structure that allows student agency to thrive—PLCs.

## Personalized Learning

To be highly effective and learning progressive, schools must identify how to create and offer a guaranteed and viable curriculum to students in a way that allows them to choose their path and pace. Stakeholders can interpret personalized learning in different ways depending on the audience and context. All too often the idea of personalization is vague and unclear, leaving administrators, teachers, parents, and, most importantly, students without a focused understanding and direction. Stakeholders often reduce personalized learning to the idea that students need to *follow their bliss*—wherever that leads—and without any commitment to essential competences.

For the sake of clarity, we define personalization in two ways: (1) through learning pathways and (2) through learning progressions—two different constructs that create an actionable framework.

## Learning Pathways

A highly effective and learning-progressive school should offer students the chance to own their learning pathways through having the choice and the opportunity to pursue their interests and passions. With personalized learning pathways, students can develop proficiency in the transdisciplinary skills essential for success in the 21st century, such as critical thinking, communication, collaboration, and creativity. Personalized learning pathways encourage students to choose their own route to meet the essential standards in ways that reflect their personal interests, strengths, and passions. With these pathways, students aren't just "following their hearts." They are developing proficiency in the transdisciplinary skills while simultaneously demonstrating mastery in other essential content areas. For example, let's say your school has a transition program for new students at the start of the school year. A learning standard might be, "Students demonstrate competent use of core technology tools at our school." A pathway approach would lay out several interest areas through which students could learn to use and master the technology tools; for example, there might be a pathway through entrepreneurship, the arts, journalism, science exploration, and sports. Students choose a personalized pathway that makes the learning more interesting and relevant to them, but they all gain competence in the same essential technology skills and tools they use within their pathway.

## Learning Progressions

Additionally, students should be able to progress through essential disciplinary outcomes by accelerating and decelerating their rate of learning based on their aptitude and learning needs, their areas of strength and weakness. Learning progressions offer students discrete steps or stages to mastery. Students demonstrate mastery at their own pace so that they are neither held back nor left behind en route to competence, and they can map where they are on the journey because the progressions are both fixed and transparent. Well-planned and communicated progressions allow students to apply their own vision, strategy, intrinsic motivation, and agency in learning. A learning progression is a school's articulated scope and sequence of learning standards—what the school and collaborative teams have decided is important for a student to know and be able to do. The only difference is that the student knows, understands, and ultimately internalizes the learning progression.

By offering both pathways and progressions, highly effective and learning-progressive schools distinguish themselves and serve students exceptionally well to be future-ready for the 21st century.

# Personalized Learning and the Real World

For more than a century, constructivist theorists have asserted the fact that students learn best when their learning connects to the real world (Dewey, 1897). The Gates Foundation (2001–2005) research suggests that an optimal learning environment includes the new 3Rs: (1) rigor, (2) relationship, and (3) relevance (as cited in Daggett, 2004). These all point to the idea that, in an effective personalized learning environment, students can explore, discover, and pursue areas of personal interest. There is no doubt that when given the opportunity to research something of genuine interest, students will dig deeper, explore further, and inquire more earnestly. This alone heightens a student's motivation and creates a positive platform for learning.

As students inquire into their areas of interest, they begin to move from exploring interests to pursuing a passion. Sometimes a passion ignites when a student is simply experimenting with a project; the joy of inquiry can set an interest ablaze. Other times, overt questions from educators like, "What really excites you?" or "If you had the opportunity, what would you spend more time doing?" can help bring hidden passions to the surface.

By utilizing different learning pathways within the same subject area, students can master the same standard in ways that interest them the most. Some learning-progressive schools also include time for students to pursue their interests. They call this time passion time, personal inquiry time, catalyst projects, senior projects, and 20 percent time. All of these experiences, regardless of their names, provide students the opportunities to identify what they want to know and be able to do, and pursue that line of inquiry to the end. An example of pathway experiences appears in greater detail in chapters 7, 8, and 9. Schools also include programs such as the International Baccalaureate Extended Essay or the AP Seminar and AP Research courses.

The International Baccalaureate and Advanced Placement Capstone Diploma have become two of the most respected college preparatory programs. Both of these programs have, at their core, opportunities (and rigorous academic criteria) for students to dive deep into areas of interest and passion.

Intentions for students using these programs can vary, including reaching core academic learning targets, learning research skills, obtaining habits of mind or habits of heart, or gaining 21st century skills (Costa & Kallick, 2014). At their core, however, they allow students to learn and develop essential transdisciplinary outcomes through a deep and rigorous pursuit of an area of interest. These authentic learning experiences' connections to the real world are critical for getting students future-ready. For example, they help students with academic pursuits after graduation, such as when, during admissions processes, colleges look for evidence that students pursued deep intellectual inquiry in an area of interest or passion. More and more colleges and universities are not only looking for well-rounded academic students but also looking for the factor that sets a student apart. They are looking for "pointy" students. Personalized learning pathway experiences give students the opportunity to do just that—show how pointy they are.

You might be wondering how the teacher's role changes in a highly effective and learning-progressive school in which students have agency over their own learning within learning pathways and learning progressions. In such schools, teachers function as learning coaches.

## Teacher as Learning Coach

To teachers, personalized learning can be a scary prospect—and for good reason. It may seem to teachers to be virtually impossible to personalize learning for large classes with students who have a variety of skill levels, interests, and needs. Thus, we posit that teachers must embrace a different role: that of learning coach. As coaches, teachers can empower students with agency to personally drive their own learning. By harnessing the power of each student, what previously was daunting becomes possible.

When educators shift to the role of learning coach, it challenges both students and teachers. This shift in role is vital, yet we must emphasize that it still values the teacher as the expert. PLCs are built on the collective knowledge of teachers. With personalized learning, teachers use knowledge to empower students to lead their learning. The teacher serves as the intellectual mentor who guides and supports. The teacher is the master craftsperson—the one who knows, but who also nurtures the apprentice.

In a learning-progressive school, the teacher is highly proactive in differentiating and tailoring teaching and learning strategies to meet individual student learning needs, interests, and learning styles. In his or her role as the facilitator of learning, the teacher moves from being largely the *sage on the stage* to what Erica McWilliam (2009) calls the *meddler in the middle*, setting up provocative learning experiences, provoking the right questions, and guiding the learning journey. This is a completely different role and requires a growth mindset, skill, and training. Teachers move from being the master teacher to becoming the master learner. If the vast majority of teachers enter the profession for the love of learning, then this approach allows them to return to this sweet spot, watching the love of learning take root in students in profound ways.

A personalized learning culture requires teachers to know and understand each student as a person and learner. Strong relationships and collaboration between the teacher and student as well as a strong sense of community within the class characterize such a culture. Teaching and learning are challenging, flexible, and adaptable and focus on critical thinking and metacognitive practices to develop stronger, deeper, independent learners.

A personalized learning culture in which teachers act as learning coaches encourages students to have agency over their learning. They are able to identify their own learning goals, ask the right questions about their learning, identify learning strategies that are in line with their learning style, self-reflect about their learning, and self-monitor their progress toward their essential learning outcomes. They see learning as a repeatable, challenging, meaningful cycle of inquiry for which they can take responsibility and that applies to real life—not just in the classroom.

## The Learning Process: A Cycle of Inquiry

The schools we observed around the world define the learning process or the cycle of inquiry in a variety of ways. In some systems, the teacher knew the process and led students through it without any overt dialogue about how it unfolded. In others, the students internalized the process and knew the stages, but didn't feel any ownership over timing or execution. In yet other systems, students actively knew and owned the process in whole or in part.

Highly effective and learning-progressive schools create structures for students to actively engage in the learning process as they own their learning. This is an intentional process and one of the primary roles and responsibilities of each teacher and collaborative team. This goes beyond students simply owning *what* they learn. Students must own *how* they learn, and *why* they learn—the learning process itself. When a student actively understands the learning process, owns it, and internalizes the process, this action challenges the student's fixed mindset, feeds his or her growth mindset, and helps the student develop grit.

As Michael Fullan and Maria Langworthy (2014) note:

> The goal is not only to master content knowledge; it is to master the learning process. Learning to learn requires that students begin to define their own learning goals and success criteria; monitor their own learning; critically examine their own work; incorporate feedback from peers, teachers, parents . . . ; and use all of this to deepen their awareness of how they function in the learning process.

There are many valid and effective structures that prove to be effective constructs to give students agency of their learning. As we explain in chapter 1, we believe the PLC process is the most promising model of research-based inquiry for educators, and in our personalized learning model, we extend the PLC process to student work.

## The PLC Process

There has never been greater consensus in education regarding school structures and instructional practices proven to best ensure student learning. Comprehensive studies of the world's best-performing school systems find that they function as PLCs (Barber, Chijioke, & Mourshed, 2010; Barber & Mourshed, 2007). Many of the most acclaimed education researchers across the globe endorse the PLC process, including Michael Fullan (as cited in DuFour & Fullan, 2013), Robert J. Marzano (DuFour & Marzano, 2011), John Hattie (as cited in DuFour, 2015), Douglas Reeves (DuFour, Reeves, & DuFour, 2018), Lawrence W. Lezotte (2005), and Mike Schmoker (2005). Likewise, most teaching and education leadership organizations endorse PLCs (DuFour, 2016). We believe that being a PLC is an essential prerequisite to becoming a highly effective and learning-progressive school and that the PLC at Work™ process that Richard DuFour, Robert Eaker, and Rebecca DuFour developed is the best way to cultivate such a transformation.

Educators in PLC schools understand that being a PLC is not participating in a program in which there is a prescribed curriculum or dictated instructional practices on a master schedule. Rather, functioning as a PLC is participating in a continuous process focused on and dedicated to a shared mission of ensuring high levels of learning for every student (DuFour et al., 2016). This focus on learning unites and guides the organization's collaborative efforts; the organization asks the question, "Will this action improve student learning?" to assess all its policies, practices, and procedures (DuFour et al., 2016).

Because individual educators cannot possibly possess all the knowledge, skills, and resources they need to ensure high levels of learning for every student, members of a PLC work collaboratively and take collective responsibility for student success. Creating this *collaborative culture* requires a PLC to shift from a traditional school structure, in which teachers work primarily in isolated classrooms, to an organization and school structure designed around collaborative teams that share responsibility for each student's success (DuFour et al., 2016). This collaboration does not happen by invitation or chance. Instead, the master schedule embeds time for frequent teacher collaboration.

In a PLC, the four critical questions guide teacher collaboration (DuFour et al., 2016):

1. What do we want all students to know and be able to do?

2. How will we know if they learn it?

3.  How will we respond when some students do not learn?

4.  How will we extend the learning for students who are already proficient?

Because these questions focus on curricular outcomes, collaborative teams form around educators who share essential learning outcomes for their students.

Finally, because members of a PLC commit to *ensuring* student success, they purposefully seek timely, relevant information—evidence of student learning—that confirms which practices are increasing student learning and which actions are not. This *results orientation* drives the school's continuous-improvement efforts. When students are not succeeding, educators commit to learning together about better practice (collective inquiry) and applying what they learn (action research) to achieve better results for their students. PLCs operate under the assumption that the key to improved learning for students is continuous job-embedded learning of the adults in the school (DuFour et al., 2016).

The three big ideas of a PLC—(1) a focus on learning, (2) a collaborative culture, and (3) a results orientation—are the foundational guiding principles of the PLC at Work process (DuFour et al., 2016). Exactly how these ideas are put into daily practice might look different from school to school. But as authors Mike Mattos, Richard DuFour, Rebecca DuFour, Robert Eaker, and Thomas W. Many (2016) clearly state:

> Imagine a school in which the educators have built consensus on the following assertions:
>
> We recognize that the fundamental purpose of our school and the reason we come to work each day is to ensure all students learn at high levels. We understand that helping all students learn requires a collective, collaborative effort rather than a series of isolated efforts. Therefore, we work in teams and constantly gather evidence of student learning for two purposes: to inform and improve our individual and collective practice and to better meet the needs of individual students through intervention or extension.
>
> Without this shared understanding of basic assumptions, every question that arises in a school can become a matter for debate based on individual opinions and personal war stories. When others accept these assumptions, they serve as filters that guide the decision-making process in a PLC. (p. 11)

We contend that it would be virtually impossible to become a highly effective and learning-progressive school if educators do not collectively commit to aligning their school's practices and procedures to these powerful guiding principles.

# The PLC Learning Process Through the Four Critical Questions

We believe that the most logical place to start in designing a learning process that emphasizes student agency is to have students engage in the same PLC inquiry process by asking the four critical questions of a PLC for themselves.

1. **What do I want to know, understand, and be able to do?** What is my learning goal?

2. **How will I demonstrate that I have learned it?** What is my evidence of learning?

3. **What will I do when I am not learning?** How will I get out of the learning pit?

4. **What will I do when I have already learned it?** What is my next learning challenge?

By asking these four questions, students are participating in a cycle of inquiry to personalize and take ownership of their learning in purposeful and concrete ways. Each student is able to articulate where he or she is at any time in the learning process.

Figure 2.1 represents the PLC learning process in which each stage of inquiry connects to one of the critical questions of a PLC. This student-owned cycle of inquiry creates the framework through which students can achieve agency over their learning process and personalize their learning.

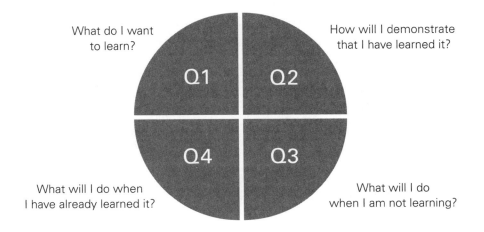

**Figure 2.1:** The PLC cycle of inquiry for students.

The key to the process is that *all* students, whether they are struggling to demonstrate mastery or are always one step ahead of their peers, receive the time and structures to own their learning. PLCs provide the ideal platform for schools to personalize students' learning experience while maintaining a core of highly effective learning.

To personalize learning in the cycle of inquiry, the teacher, acting as a learning coach, maintains an important role. The teacher must communicate or make available the learning outcomes in an age-appropriate way so all learners clearly understand how they must demonstrate proficiency in their learning. Diagnostic information is still vital, and the teacher supports the students as they reflect on their results, identifying areas where they are already proficient and opportunities for growth. Using diagnostic assessment data, the student partners with the teacher to create a personalized learning plan to, at minimum, attain proficiency in all standard areas, but also to allow for personalization and exploration of his or her interests as a learner. The teacher and student develop a formative assessment calendar to reflect on the student's evidence of learning and to ensure the student is progressing in his or her personal learning plan. Ultimately, the teacher team remains in the role of evaluator as it uses the entirety of the evidence to ensure the student has learned the intended curriculum. As the student becomes more independent and internalizes the process of learning, he or she is able to create, develop, and take more ownership of the process, and the teacher moves from guide to mentor.

## Learning as the Constant

In highly effective and learning-progressive schools, learning is the constant and time is the variable. PLC schools know this to be at the heart of the mission of PLCs: all students can learn at high levels (DuFour et al., 2016). When personalized learning progressions are in place, and students understand and internalize them, students are then held accountable to clearly articulated learning outcomes that the school, district, or state (or province) establishes. These outcomes do not restrict students to a strict *unit of content = unit of time* model. Instead, students will progress through the learning at their own pace by demonstrating mastery of each essential disciplinary learning outcome as they are able.

The success of such a strategy for learning is evident in the gaming industry, which has mastered the concept of personalized learning. Designers build games with specific levels or stages for participants to master. Gamers know exactly when they have reached a new level and what they need to do to conquer the next level. The gaming industry, however, does not require gamers to wait until all gamers have mastered a level before moving to the next one. Neither are gamers left behind just because other gamers have conquered a level before others unlock the same challenge. While the levels of mastery are fixed, each gamer owns his or her pace, progressing through each new stage at a rate optimal for him or her. This personalized approach keeps the gamer engaged and challenged appropriately so that he or she willingly spends the time necessary to perfect the required skills. It's the only way to qualify for the next level! How do we tap into that intrinsic motivation in education so school stays relevant to this and future generations who see choice as part of their natural habitat for learning? Schools certainly have a thing or two to learn from the gaming industry in this regard. Whether planting crops in agricultural sim games or capturing castles or protecting territory in war games, young people believe the levels are worth challenging and mastering, and they learn a lot in the process—without adults guiding their every move.

The mastery of essential learning outcomes is central to the personalized learning-progressive model. However, to be successful in a 21st century global society, students must have skills and dispositions that go beyond a traditional content-based education. School should continue to emphasize core knowledge, but students must also develop new thinking, self-management skills, and dispositions such as critical thinking, creativity, collaboration, communication, cultural competence, and the character to navigate and flourish in a world of rapid change and expanding possibilities.

Each day, students must know where they are in their learning progression and what they need to learn next. As we have traveled the globe speaking with teachers, it is clear to us that many educators long to create such a learning environment for their students. Luckily, advances in technology make such models possible for the first time, stretching the capacity of students and teachers to track individual progress in new and innovative, real-time ways. These possibilities now alter the landscape, increasing the ways we can learn, record, assess, and report learning.

Many schools have become highly effective learning institutions with the successful implementation of the PLC process. The data and research are clear: the PLC model provides a powerful way to allow students to learn at high levels. Our goal is to empower students with agency in order to extend the foundational work of PLCs to even greater success. We believe strongly that when student agency is built into the work of PLCs, student learning will be limitless. The larger question is this: Are we up for the challenge of reconstructing our schools and our teaching to support maximum learning for all students? In the next chapter, we show how schools can use this framework to support the highest levels of learning in highly effective and learning-progressive schools.

## Rate Your Progression

Knowing what you know about our changing world and its impact on what is important for students to know and be able to do, how must your school change in order to meet these real-world, future needs?

## Tips for Transformation

The following are five tips to transform school culture.

1.  Highly effective and learning-progressive schools must create structures for students to actively engage in the learning process as they own their learning.

2.  The most logical place to start to give agency within a personalized learning structure is to allow students to engage in the same PLC process as collaborative teams by asking the four critical questions of the PLC for themselves.

    a.  **What do I want to know, understand, and be able to do?** What is my learning goal?

    b.  **How will I demonstrate that I have learned it?** What is my evidence of learning?

    c.  **What will I do when I am not learning**? How will I get out of the learning pit?

    d.  **What will I do when I have already learned it**? What is my next learning challenge?

3.  Students must see learning as a repeatable, challenging, meaningful cycle of inquiry for which they can take responsibility and that applies to their real life—not just in the classroom.

4.  Personalized pathways give students the opportunity to develop proficiency in the transdisciplinary skills identified as essential for survival and success in the 21st century.

5.  Personalized learning progressions offer students discrete steps or stages to mastery. Students can demonstrate mastery at their own pace so that they are neither held back nor left behind as they work toward competence and map their progress.

## Questions to Consider

Consider the following four questions as you begin your transformation to a highly effective and learning-progressive school.

1.  **The learning:** What are the important learnings for me in this chapter? For my school? What am I inspired to know and be able to do?

2.  **The evidence:** What are we already doing that aligns with this paradigm? What would change in my school and professional experience if we further embrace and implement it?

3.  **The learning pit:** What obstacles would we face if we were to try or to further this approach? What strategies could we use to experience breakthroughs?

4.  **The lever:** What would we need to accelerate the change process?

# 3

# Systems of Collaboration and Support for Personalized Learning

Consider for a moment how parents teach their child how to drive a car. They don't wait for their son or daughter to turn the legal age to drive, then toss him or her the keys to the family car and say, "You're an adult now . . . the open road awaits!" Instead, parents start teaching their child the skills and behaviors the new driver needs to safely drive an automobile long before he or she ever gets to sit behind the wheel. Some skills are disciplinary skills related to driving a vehicle—like rules of the road—but students might first practice them on a bicycle in the driveway. Some of the skills are transdisciplinary, like drawing a conclusion that even though the posted speed sign allows a maximum speed of sixty-five miles per hour, the current road conditions would indicate one should drive more slowly. Finally, some of the essential skills are behaviors—like how to peacefully solve a disagreement. Failure to master such behavior can lead to an act of deadly road rage.

As a young person begins to master the skills, critical thinking, and behavior he or she needs to safely drive a car, the student driver is put into controlled environments to practice. The new driver first drives with a permit, with an experienced driver in the car ready to provide advice and coaching, and to even take the wheel if needed. Even after a teen earns his or her driver's license, a parent might place restrictions on when and where the new driver can go. This gradual release of responsibility, from the experienced adult to the novice, is carefully coordinated to give the young driver the best chance to survive and thrive.

Likewise, while the goal of a highly effective and learning-progressive school is to have students personalize their learning through student agency, the transition of responsibility and ownership in answering the four critical PLC questions must be released gradually. We can't stress this point enough: while the ultimate goal of a highly effective and learning-progressive school is for each student to take responsibility for his or her own learning, *this outcome does not abdicate the school's responsibility to ensure every student's success.* As educators, we create the learning environment. We identify the essential learning outcomes. We plan the instruction. We monitor each student's learning. And ultimately, we provide the safety net when students fail in their initial attempts to master the skills they need to be successful.

With such rigorous learning expectations required for every student, creating an effective system of support is a necessity in a highly effective and learning-progressive school. We observed that these schools aligned their PLC practices to support such an approach and implemented a multitiered system of supports, such as RTI, to ensure students achieve at high levels.

# Aligning PLC Practices to Progressive Learning Outcomes

The first of the four critical questions of a PLC—What do we want all students to know and be able to do?—determines the learning outcomes that all students must master to learn at high levels. The answer to this question drives the school's instruction, assessment, intervention, and extension practices. To this end, we identify three types of learning outcomes for a highly effective and learning-progressive school: (1) essential disciplinary outcomes, (2) essential transdisciplinary outcomes, and (3) essential personalized learning outcomes.

## Essential Disciplinary Outcomes

All students must master specific content knowledge as they progress through grade levels. As Craig D. Jerald (2009) states in *Defining a 21st Century Education*:

> Subject matter knowledge and basic skills are important building blocks for the broader competencies gaining value in the 21st century . . . being able to think critically about a topic or solve a problem in a particular domain demands sufficient background knowledge about it. And an important aspect of creativity is making connections across domains of knowledge— something that is impossible unless someone knows enough in different domains to make such a connection. (p. 31)

The following outcomes represent the traditional subject-specific content knowledge that students must master at each grade level. In the primary grades, these disciplinary outcomes begin by focusing on foundational skills.

- **Reading:** Including phonological awareness, phonics, fluency, vocabulary, and comprehension

- **Mathematics:** Including mastering the concepts of rounding, ordering, and comparing numbers; time and money; adding, subtracting, multiplying, and dividing numbers; fractions and decimals; rates, ratios, and proportions; algebraic expressions and equations; measurement and geometry; and statistics and probability

- **Writing:** Including ideas, organization, and conventions

- **English language:** Including functionally based oral and written expression (If the primary language for instruction is another language besides English, then this native language would be the desired outcome. If a student does not know the language of instruction, then the student's learning would be negatively impacted.)

- **Subject-specific content knowledge:** Including mathematics, science, social studies, health and fitness, and the arts

These foundational skills are critical to a student's ability to gain essential content knowledge and continue learning.

## Essential Transdisciplinary Outcomes

Beyond subject-specific essential disciplinary outcomes, it is essential that students master the critical-thinking skills, behaviors, and dispositions they need to apply what they learn to future situations, problems, and environments, as well as to adapt and create new ideas and connections. These skills and behaviors are not subject specific; they should be taught across the curriculum and grade levels. Clearly defining these essential academic skills and behaviors, and coordinating the teaching of them across the school, will require frequent, focused transdisciplinary collaboration. Examples of these academic skills and behaviors could include:

- Drawing inferences and conclusions from texts

- Analyzing conflicting source documents

- Supporting arguments with evidence

- Solving complex problems with no obvious answer

- Building metacognition—knowledge and beliefs about thinking

- Self-monitoring to plan and prepare for learning

- Initiating and maintaining interest in tasks through motivation

- Learning techniques for organization and memorization of knowledge

- Growing volition—the efforts and techniques needed to stay motivated and engaged in learning

## Essential Personalized Outcomes

The ultimate goal of a learning-progressive school is to ensure that every student masters the student-agency skills he or she needs to personalize learning to achieve individual, lifelong goals. Achieving this outcome requires students to master essential disciplinary and transdisciplinary skills, then apply and extend this learning into curriculum and learning targets that students drive with their interests, passions, and goals.

For example, a student might determine that he or she wants to explore the topic of forensic psychology. This interest could be driven by intellectual curiosity that could potentially lead to a future career. As it is unlikely that this topic is required curriculum, the student would work with the faculty to co-create learning opportunities and outcomes focused in this area of personal interest. To successfully complete this personalized learning outcome, the student would have to utilize and apply disciplinary and transdisciplinary essential skills. The student would apply the disciplinary skills of analytical reading and writing to study psychology, as well as transdisciplinary skills like drawing conclusions. Equally important, the student would need to demonstrate essential academic behaviors, including self-monitoring and volition. Providing student opportunities for personalized learning without ensuring a strong foundation of disciplinary and interdisciplinary skills would be setting students up for failure.

Designing such outcomes requires collaborative structures within teams of teachers in highly effective and learning-progressive schools in addition to a multitiered system of supports (MTSS) for students.

# Designing Collaborative Structures for Progressive Learning Outcomes

Collaborative teams are the engine that drives the PLC process. Because student learning is the focus of this collaboration, creating teams with membership that shares essential learning outcomes is critical. To this end, we recommend that highly effective and learning-progressive schools create three types of team structures that reflect the three learning outcomes: (1) disciplinary collaborative teams, (2) transdisciplinary collaborative teams, and (3) personalized learning teams.

## Disciplinary Collaborative Teams

Disciplinary teams consist of team members who share essential disciplinary standards. At most schools, these teams would be grade-level teams in the elementary grades, and subject- or course-specific teams at the secondary level. These teams take lead responsibility for:

- Identifying the absolutely essential academic content standards that all students must master for their grade level or course (These outcomes do not represent all the curriculum that will be part of a student's core instruction, but instead the guaranteed and viable curriculum that a student must master to prepare for the next grade or course.)

- Teaching the identified essential learning outcomes

- Gathering evidence of learning for each student on these essential standards, and using these data to reflect on the effectiveness of their individual and collective teaching

- Being part of a schoolwide, systematic process to help intervene when students struggle, and extending student learning when they need it

Because students in a highly effective and learning-progressive school will progress through the essential curriculum at differing rates, there must also be vertical collaboration and articulation across disciplinary teams. Clearly defining learning progressions of essential standards is critical to personalized learning outcomes.

## Transdisciplinary Collaborative Teams

In addition to disciplinary teams, the school should form logical transdisciplinary teams to identify the essential cross-disciplinary skills and behaviors that all students must master for future success. These teams could take many different forms, based on the size of the school, student needs, and the school's level of competency in the PLC process. Team structures could include:

- **Vertical teams**—Vertical teams consist of team members who span multiple grade levels, and they focus on identifying transdisciplinary skills that are taught across grade levels. For example, drawing inferences and conclusions is a higher-level-thinking skill that is taught not in a single grade but rather across multiple years. Determining common vocabulary, specific rigor expectations for each grade, assessments, and interventions would drive the work of this team.

- **Interdisciplinary teams**—Like a vertical team, this team identifies essential transdisciplinary skills that stretch across subjects. For example, argumentation is an essential skill that can be taught across disciplines. This team would identify these skills and determine common vocabulary, specific rigor expectations, common assessments, and interventions.

- **Task force**—A task force convenes for a specific transdisciplinary topic, such as determination of essential schoolwide academic and social behaviors. We have seen schools successfully create a school task force, made up of cross-grade or cross-disciplinary team members to study essential academic behaviors. This team would identify these skills, determine common vocabulary, identify specific rigor expectations, develop assessments to monitor student progress, and lead interventions.

- **Full faculty**—The full faculty meet when it is necessary to engage the entire staff, such as in applying the four critical questions to transdisciplinary skills and behaviors.

As transdisciplinary teams identify essential cross-disciplinary skills and behaviors, it is important to include disciplinary teams in order to determine how teachers can use their essential disciplinary content as a vehicle to teach essential transdisciplinary skills and behaviors. To this end, it is likely that faculty members will be part of both disciplinary and transdisciplinary teams. For example, a high school might have geometry teachers form a disciplinary team that focuses on the essential mathematical skills a student must learn in this course for future success in mathematics. Concurrently, one member of the geometry team might serve on a site transdisciplinary team that has identified argumentation as an essential cross-disciplinary skill. The teacher would report back to the geometry team, sharing the common vocabulary for this transdisciplinary skill. As solving proofs in geometry requires students to demonstrate argumentation, this disciplinary team can align and support geometry students in learning this larger, higher-level-thinking skill.

## Personalized Learning Teams

Since the goal of a learning-progressive school is to empower each student to personalize, direct, and take ultimate responsibility for his or her own learning, schools must include students in answering the four critical questions of a PLC to achieve this goal. This means there must be time for teachers—and teacher teams—to collaborate with individual students. The membership and structure of these teams will vary greatly based on the personalized learning goals of each student. For example, if a student wanted to create a personalized learning goal within a specific disciplinary subject, then the disciplinary team would serve as the personalized learning team to help guide and support the student's efforts. If the personalized learning goal required cross-disciplinary content and skills, then a transdisciplinary team would best serve this outcome. Finally, in some cases, a specific teacher advisor might serve as the primary faculty member to team with a specific student in creating and coordinating personalized learning outcomes for the specific student. Specific examples of these team structures will be provided in later chapters.

These three types of teams do not work in isolation. They all share the same mission—high levels of learning for every student—and each represents a specific set of learning outcomes students need to achieve this goal. Over time, we find that highly effective and learning-progressive schools combine these teams into more fluid teaming structures based on each student's needs. Examples of these fluid structures appear in subsequent chapters.

In addition to these specific PLC teaming structures to support students, highly effective and learning-progressive schools use a system of multitiered intervention, such as RTI, to support students as they move from initial core instruction to mastery.

## Implementing Response to Intervention

So how does a school ensure that every student learns at high levels when all students don't enter school with the same prior knowledge, skills, and parental support? When it comes to how educators should respond when students struggle in school, the research and evidence are conclusive—RTI is the right way to intervene (Buffum, Mattos, & Malone, 2018). Also known as an MTSS, RTI is a systematic process to ensure every student receives the additional time and support he or she needs to learn at high levels.

Austin Buffum, Mike Mattos, and Chris Weber (2012) note:

> RTI's underlying premise is that schools should not delay providing help for struggling students until they fall far enough behind to qualify for special education, but instead should provide timely, targeted, systematic interventions to all students who demonstrate the need. (p. xiii)

Based on his meta-analysis of more than eighty thousand studies relating to the factors inside and outside of school that impact student learning, researcher John Hattie (2009, 2012) finds that RTI ranks in the top-three education practices that prove to best increase student achievement. When implemented well, RTI has an exceptional average yearly impact rate of 1.29 standard deviation (Hattie, 2016).

To put this in perspective, consider the following.

- A one standard deviation (1.0) increase is typically associated with advancing student achievement within two to three years (Hattie, 2009).

- Based on longitudinal studies, the yearly typical impact rate of a classroom teacher's instruction ranges between 0.15 and 0.40 standard deviation growth (Hattie, 2009). This means a school that successfully implements RTI leverages a process that is considerably more effective than a school that leaves it up to individual, isolated teachers to meet students' instructional needs.

- The greatest home or environmental factor that impacts student learning is a family's economic status. Students who come from more affluent homes—defined as middle class or higher—gain a yearly academic benefit of 0.57 standard deviation growth per year (Hattie, 2009). RTI's impact rate of 1.29—more than twice as powerful as what some students might receive at home each night—provides educators a proven, powerful tool to close the largest achievement gap.

In their work on RTI, Buffum et al. (2018) identify four objectives that a system of interventions that is multitiered and systematic must achieve.

1. **Students must have access to essential curriculum as part of their instruction program:** This access supports the ultimate goal of a learning-focused school is to ensure every student ends each year having acquired the essential skills, knowledge, and behaviors he or she requires for future success. This means that in a highly effective and learning-progressive school, there would not be a less rigorous, remedial track of learning for some students.

2. **Flexible time is embedded within the school day:** Because all students do not learn the same way or at the same speed, this time is to provide students with extra time and support in learning the essential skills, knowledge, and behaviors they require for future success. Likewise, teachers can also use this flexible time to extend the learning of students who have mastered their current core essential curriculum. Finally, students must receive this help without missing instruction in new essential core curriculum.

3. **Intensive remediation is available:** Some students enter each school year lacking the skills, knowledge, and behaviors they should have mastered in prior years. These students need intensive remediation to catch up on these

prerequisite skills. Again, students must receive this help without missing instruction in new essential core curriculum.

4. **Those students who need them will require all three objectives.**

   a. Access to new essential curriculum

   b. Interventions to learn this curriculum

   c. Intensive remediation in prior skills

The RTI process includes three tiers that focus on core instruction and two levels of intervention when students do not master the learning outcomes.

Because all students do not learn the same way or at the same speed, the school creates a flexible schedule to provide both additional time and support in learning essential curriculum and extension or provide acceleration opportunities for students who have learned. Some students might fall behind on an essential learning progression, thus entering a school year lacking prerequisite skills, knowledge, and behaviors they need to learn new essential curriculum. Subsequently, the school day is designed so that some students receive intensive remediation to catch the students up in these prior skills and behaviors without missing new essential curriculum.

RTI is a systematic process, which means that every student is guaranteed this support. Specifically, this support:

- Occurs during the instructional day, so obstacles such as transportation or parental approval are not necessary for students to receive help

- Does not require a student to qualify for assistance due to an identified disability, an economic status of the parent, or any other criteria

- Is not dependent on which teacher a student receives for core instruction

We assume that for many educators, viewing RTI as a process to support students in the most rigorous curriculum is a new concept. Traditionally, schools viewed interventions as a tool to aid low-achieving, at-risk students. Yet, at its core, RTI is a systematic process to differentiate time and instruction to ensure student learning. There is no reason why the learning outcomes a school's RTI process targets could not be rigorous.

# Gradually Releasing Responsibility

Like the opening example of the chapter regarding teaching your child how to drive, putting students in the driver's seat to guide their own learning must be a systematic process in which responsibility is gradually released from the trained educators to the learners. The outcome is best achieved when the four critical questions of the PLC at

Work process are released to students in reverse order. Student engagement in these questions, revised to represent student agency, is as follows.

4. **What will I do when I have already learned it?** This question represents extending learning when students have mastered essential curriculum. These students have learned essential content and skills, which is a prerequisite to applying what they have learned to personalized areas of interest, with a greater depth of application, and between disciplines. Beginning in the earliest grades of school, teacher teams can create opportunities for students to have a voice and choice in how to extend their learning.

3. **What will I do when I am not learning?** As students begin to accept responsibility for their learning, they must be taught how to self-advocate when they need additional time and support to learn essential disciplinary and transdisciplinary skills or extended learning. However, student agency should not place students into a "sink or swim" environment, but instead teach students how to seek help if they begin to struggle.

2. **How will I demonstrate that I have learned it?** For the next steps in gradual release, students have choice and voice in how they can demonstrate their learning of teacher team–determined essential learning outcomes. Teaching students how to do this will require students to understand learning targets and assessment criteria and to self-monitor their learning, both skills needed to reach the ultimate learning goal of answering critical question 1.

1. **What do I want to know, understand, and be able to do?** Students answering this question is the ultimate goal of personalized learning and student agency. Because the previous three questions are released first, students have been "student drivers" who have practiced how to apply personal choice to extended learning outcomes, how to advocate for help when they get stuck, how to break learning outcomes down into specific learning targets, and how to assess and monitor their progress. Equally important, the teachers have ensured that students have mastered the essential prerequisite disciplinary and interdisciplinary content and skills needed to independently drive their learning.

One way to capture and document the cycle of inquiry and have students articulate where they are at in the learning process is with the worksheet in figure 3.1. This useful guide is helpful as collaborative teams look for ways to engage all students in the learning process. This process is not a step-by-step formula; rather, schools can adapt or modify it to meet each student's and team's needs at various stages.

**Unit of study:** _____

**Student name:** _____

### Stage 1: Learning Target—What Do I Want to Know and Be Able to Do?

Prior knowledge:

Facts I need to know:

Skills I need to be able to do:

Context I need to understand:

### Stage 2: Assessment—How Will I Show That I Have Learned It?

Formative assessment 1:

Formative assessment 2:

Summative assessment:

Authentic project:

**Figure 3.1:** Student meaning-making worksheet.

continued ➔

**Stage 3: Intervention—What Will I Do If I Am Not Learning?**

Resources available for help:

Strategies to get out of the learning pit:

Time students need to relearn:

Interventions:

**Stage 4: Extension—What Will I Do If I Have Already Learned It?**

Next step in the learning progression:

Connections to other things I know:

Deeper understanding of this topic:

Interest- and passion-based exploration:

*Visit* **go.SolutionTree.com/PLCbooks** *to download a free reproducible version of this figure.*

Just as students need a gradual process to practice and gain the skills required to master progressive learning outcomes, schools and educators need the same systematic support to become a highly effective learning-progressive school. We believe the gradual release of the four critical questions is a good way for teacher teams—and schools—to focus their collaborative efforts. Jumping straight into having students co-create curriculum is daunting, but having students have some choice and voice in extended learning opportunities is not uncommon in most schools. So, this is a great place for teacher teams to start. As teams get better at addressing question 4, considering how to teach students self-advocating skills is a next logical step. This gradual release—for educators and students—can make the journey more doable and successful.

PLC practices, collaborative structures, a system of intervention and extension, and gradual release of responsibility are all critical pieces of highly effective and learning-progressive schools, along with the elements we discussed in the previous chapter: learning pathways, learning progressions, and the cycle of inquiry. Figure 3.2 (page 52) provides an overview of these various elements and how they interact to provide students with agency for their learning in a personalized learning environment.

# Future-Proofing Students

As we have traveled the globe visiting schools that are actively attempting to create highly effective and learning-progressive schools for their students, it is clear that the most innovative schools have put structures in place to facilitate teacher collaboration, clear learning targets, personalized learning structures, and intervention and acceleration strategies.

We believe that PLCs and RTI represent the best organizing structures to empower student agency and to engage the learner in the learning process and that schools can use them to transform the current educational paradigm in order to future-proof our students and reach the highest levels of engagement and learning for all students. PLC and RTI are complementary processes designed to produce the same outcome—high levels of student learning. PLCs create the foundation schools need to build a highly effective system of interventions.

Ultimately, if the goal of highly effective and learning-progressive schools is to prepare students for a world that will require collaboration and continuous learning, then shouldn't educators commit to creating, experiencing, and modeling the same conditions within their schools? In the remainder of this book, we dig deeper into how to structure schools in order to ensure students learn the disciplinary, transdisciplinary, and student-agency skills they need for future success.

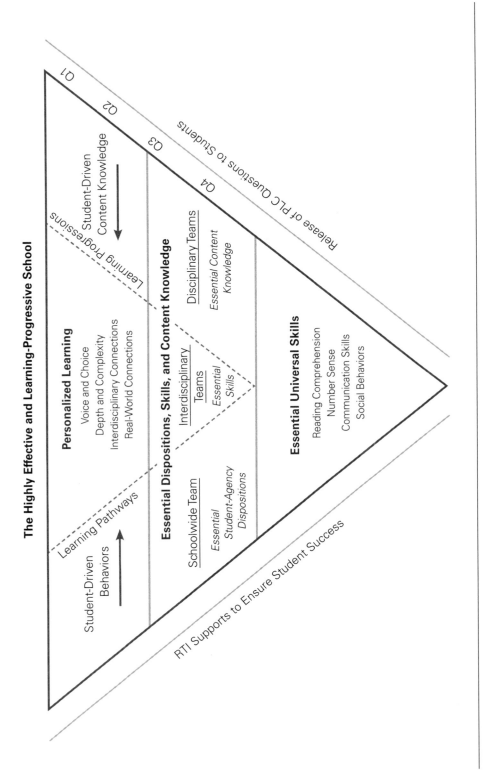

**Figure 3.2:** The elements of a highly effective and learning-progressive school.

## Rate Your Progression

How do you need to evolve the structure and composition of your collaborative teams to address the new answers to the first critical question?

## Tips for Transformation

The following are five tips to transform school culture.

1. Individual educators cannot possess all the knowledge, skills, and resources they need to ensure high levels of learning for every student. Members of a PLC work collaboratively and take collective responsibility for student success.

2. Collaboration in a PLC is driven by the first of four critical questions: *What do we want our students to know and be able to do?* Answering this question determines the learning outcomes that all students must master to learn at high levels, and drives the school's instruction, assessment, intervention, and extension practices.

3. Essential disciplinary outcomes represent the traditional subject-specific content knowledge that students must master at each grade level. In the primary grades, these disciplinary outcomes focus on foundational skills.

4. Essential transdisciplinary outcomes are the critical-thinking skills, behaviors, and dispositions students need to apply what they have learned to future situations, problems, and environments, as well as to adapt and create new ideas and connections.

5. Personalized learning outcomes are the ultimate goal of a highly effective and learning-progressive school—to ensure that every student has agency to personalize his or her learning to achieve individual, lifelong goals.

## Questions to Consider

Consider the following four questions as you begin your transformation to a highly effective and learning-progressive school.

1.  **The learning:** What are the important learnings for me in this chapter? For my school? What am I inspired to know and be able to do?

2.  **The evidence:** What are we already doing that aligns with this paradigm? What would change in my school and professional experience if we further embrace and implement it?

3.  **The learning pit:** What obstacles would we face if we were to try or to further this approach? What strategies could we use to experience breakthroughs?

4.  **The lever:** What would we need to accelerate the change process?

# PART TWO

# Adapting the Four Critical Questions

# 4

# Teacher-Led Instruction and Release of Responsibility for Essential Disciplinary Learning Outcomes

Walk into any school functioning as a PLC, anywhere in the world, and you will notice very quickly that the educators have an unfaltering commitment to ensuring that all of their students learn at high levels. Walk up to a group of teachers sitting around a table, and you will more than likely hear them working on one of the four critical questions. You may witness teachers working collaboratively to design an effective common formative assessment, or identifying students who are struggling on a particular standard and developing a creative intervention plan for that student. We have had the collective privilege of visiting dozens, if not hundreds, of these PLC exemplar schools. And every time we do, we are convinced that they are doing the right work, in the right way, for the students they serve.

A belief that all students can achieve at high levels is a prerequisite for building a highly effective school focused on learning. Collaborative teacher teams articulate what it means for students to succeed at high levels if such a school is to become highly effective and learning progressive (the essential disciplinary learning outcomes). To guarantee all students master these essential disciplinary learning outcomes, we recommend a teacher-led learning approach. In this approach, teachers answer the first three critical questions of a PLC and release responsibility to students for answering the fourth critical question. Disciplinary learning teams describe the essential disciplinary learning outcomes they expect students to master, determine how they will know if students have learned, decide what they will do to intervene when students have not learned, and then lead students in gradually gaining responsibility to decide what to do when they have learned.

Ensuring that students master the essential disciplinary learning outcomes also requires that schools implement an MTSS, such as RTI, that provides all students access to core instruction and intervention to master required outcomes. In this chapter, we explore the work of essential disciplinary learning teams in answering the four critical questions, providing students with intervention to ensure mastery, and releasing control to students to promote student agency.

# Essential Disciplinary Learning Outcomes

At every developmental level or grade level, there is a set of knowledge and skills students require to independently access and contribute to the guaranteed and viable curriculum. These essential outcomes can include academic content knowledge or expected social behaviors that facilitate learning. These grade-level, subject-area competencies are essential for students to learn, make connections with, and apply. Without mastering core academic content knowledge and skills, students will struggle to become independent learners able to access transdisciplinary and personalized learning outcomes. (We discuss these in the following chapter, page 69, and chapter 6, page 87.)

Teachers—teacher teams, specifically—lead the process of answering the four critical questions of a PLC for essential disciplinary learning. While the teacher is ultimately responsible for ensuring that all students learn the essential outcomes, the pedagogical approach teachers utilize changes to maximize learning. As students move through each learning outcome, student agency becomes increasingly important and necessary.

When targeting essential disciplinary outcomes, the collaborative teacher team is responsible for the path and pace of learning. The team must ensure that it teaches the guaranteed and viable curriculum and that all students are able to demonstrate mastery of the intended learning outcomes. Teams do this by asking and answering the four critical questions of a PLC (DuFour et al., 2016).

As we discussed in the previous chapter, disciplinary teams consist of team members who share essential disciplinary outcomes. At most schools, grade-level collaborative teams in the elementary grades and subject- or course-specific collaborative teams at the secondary level would most likely comprise these disciplinary teams. A narrative of a high-functioning disciplinary collaborative team may look something like the following.

> *A grade 5 team deconstructs the academic standards into discrete learning outcomes that connect to larger enduring understandings. The team then determines the level of performance students must achieve to attain proficiency, and also maps the pathway to proficiency with specific performance descriptors grouped into proficiency bands. Prior to the start of the unit, the teachers use diagnostic assessments to identify student needs. The team develops a sequence of highly differentiated instruction for the students to progress through the curriculum. Individual teachers monitor learning closely, and continue to adjust instruction to maximize student learning. Periodically, the teachers administer common formative assessments and use these data to identify individual student needs, adjust instruction, and determine the most effective strategies. This pattern repeats until the unit is complete and the team administers a common summative assessment, which connects the learning outcomes to the enduring understandings. The team uses the summative assessment results to determine which students need additional time and support, providing continued intervention until all students have attained proficiency.*

This narrative shows a high-performing disciplinary collaborative team that accepts student learning as the fundamental purpose. Students are likely progressing well in this team's curriculum; yet the inherent challenge is that the teacher team is carrying out the metacognitive and reflective processes that are so vital in cultivating the skills and habits necessary to become a lifelong learner. To become a highly effective and learning-progressive school, teams must understand that there are learning outcomes (transdisciplinary and personal learning outcomes) that go beyond essential disciplinary learning outcomes. We elaborate on these outcomes in the next two chapters.

## Teacher Collaboration Focused on the Mastery of Essential Disciplinary Learning Outcomes

Teachers are responsible for delivering instruction that ensures proficiency of the guaranteed and viable curriculum. Disciplinary collaborative team meetings give teacher teams the opportunity to ask and answer the four critical questions of the PLC. As teams aspire to new learning outcomes for students, the collaborative team's composition will evolve from essential disciplinary outcomes to a transdisciplinary team and then to a personalized learning team.

These teams must have protected time to collaborate. For students to maximize disciplinary learning outcomes, PLCs should structure teacher collaboration time as weekly meetings with forty-five minutes to one hour of uninterrupted dedicated meeting time.

## Critical Question 1

What do we want all students to know and be able to do? The answer to this first question establishes clarity and focus for the guaranteed and viable curriculum. It determines the essential disciplinary learning outcomes students will master. Teams must do more than look at the school's curriculum guide or the previous year's course syllabus (although those are great places to start); rather, teams must really wrestle with what they believe students should know and be able to do. As part of answering critical question 1, the collaborative team is identifying proficiency standards, unwrapping each standard, identifying the learning target for each unit of instruction, and rewording each learning target in student-friendly language. For a deeper look at the steps to take while answering critical question 1, see *Learning by Doing* (DuFour et al., 2016).

## Critical Question 2

How will we know if they learn it, or rather, how will we know when our students learn the essential disciplinary outcomes? The research is quite clear (Hattie, 2014) that one of the most powerful learning tools to answer this second critical question is a well-crafted common formative assessment that aligns to each learning outcome, an assessment that gives the student and the teacher actionable intelligence on the student's progress toward proficiency of the intended learning target. Disciplinary collaborative teams also determine what artifacts teachers will accept as evidence that students learn what they are supposed to learn or can do what they are supposed to be able to do. For teams, question 2 sets the stage for meaningful conversations about teaching practice, interventions, and extensions. Collaborative teams should utilize the full range of assessment practices available to best assess student learning; there are many options beyond traditional pencil-and-paper tests, multiple-choice tests, or fill-in-the-blank assessments. Teachers wishing to assess essential disciplinary learning outcomes can utilize a whole host of authentic assessment strategies, including oral assessments, essays, research papers, collaborative student projects, and presentations.

## Critical Question 3

How will we respond when some students do not learn? If students are not demonstrating mastery of the essential disciplinary learning outcomes, it is the responsibility of the disciplinary collaborative team to ensure that *all* students reach the desired level of proficiency. When students struggle to reach the desired level of proficiency, the school must have systems and structures (such as RTI) in place to intervene. As mentioned in chapter 3, Hattie's (2009) meta-analysis finds an effect size greater than one standard deviation when educators implement RTI effectively. This makes RTI one of the most powerful strategies to ensure that all students learn at high levels. As we mentioned in the previous chapter, there are two defining characteristics of RTI: it is a *multitiered* and *systematic* process. In the section following critical question 4, we elaborate on the components of a well-crafted RTI system and how highly effective schools use such a system to ensure that students master essential disciplinary learning outcomes.

## Critical Question 4

The fourth critical question of a PLC asks, "How will we extend the learning for students who are already proficient?" With essential disciplinary learning outcomes, the fourth question is the simplest place to give students agency over their own learning because at this stage, the student has already demonstrated proficiency of the essential disciplinary learning outcome. We recommend that teachers give students the opportunity to personalize question 4: What will I do when I have already learned it? Specifically, what do *I* want or need to learn next?

Giving students agency over their learning is simplest (and safest) with the most fluent and proficient learners in a classroom, and these students are often some of the most-forgotten students in classrooms. They get high marks and might appear to be engaged as they participate in class, but often the curriculum doesn't challenge them to learn at an even higher level. These students often become bored with school and sometimes act out in inappropriate ways, just to pass time.

When focused on essential disciplinary learning outcomes, a collaborative team often takes responsibility to scaffold the extension of learning for students. It is important to note that when educators traditionally scaffold instruction, the teacher takes on the cognitive demand of the learning. In a teacher-led learning environment, teacher scaffolding should clearly delineate the process of learning while allowing the student to embrace and feel challenged by the cognitive load. As students grow in metacognition and autonomy, the teacher provides less scaffolding of the process, and allows the learner to fully implement both the process and the cognitive demand of the learning extension. (We elaborate on strategies to challenge students while providing student agency on page 64.)

# RTI and the Mastery of Essential Disciplinary Learning Outcomes

There is a point in every unit of study when most students demonstrate mastery of the unit's essential learning outcomes, and the teacher will need to proceed to the next topic. But because some students may not master the essential curriculum (Tier 1) by the end of the unit, the school must dedicate time to provide these students additional support to master this essential grade-level curriculum *without missing critical new core instruction*. This supplemental help to master grade-level curriculum is the purpose of Tier 2 in RTI. Figure 4.1 shows the purposes of Tier 1 and Tier 2.

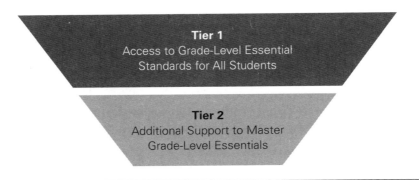

**Figure 4.1:** Tiers 1 and 2 of RTI.

Many traditional RTI approaches advocate that the key to Tier 1 is effective first instruction. We don't disagree with this, but this teaching must include instruction on the skills, knowledge, and behaviors that a student must acquire this year to be prepared for next year. Unfortunately, many schools deem their students most at risk as incapable of mastering these outcomes, so schools pull out those students or place them in Tier 3 interventions that replace their core instruction with remedial course-work. So regardless of if the initial teaching is done well, if a student's core instruction focuses on below-grade-level outcomes, then the student will learn well below grade level. The fundamental purpose of RTI is to ensure all students learn essential disciplinary outcomes at high levels—at grade level or better each year—so schools must teach all students at grade level. Every student might not leave each school year having mastered *every* grade-level standard, but every student must master the essential learning outcomes the school deems indispensable for future success.

Neither the size of the intervention group nor the duration of the intervention determines Tier 2. Instead, the targeted learning outcomes define it. Supplemental help should focus on providing targeted students with the additional time and support they need to master the specific skills, knowledge, and behaviors identified at Tier 1 to be absolutely essential for a student's future success. Classroom teachers should be actively involved at Tier 2, as these outcomes directly relate to their areas of expertise. Because supplemental interventions focus on very specific learning targets, placement into Tier 2 interventions must be timely, targeted, flexible, and most likely aligned to classroom or team-developed common formative assessments.

If a school provides students access to essential disciplinary outcomes and effective initial teaching during Tier 1 core instruction, and targeted supplemental academic and behavioral help in meeting these standards at Tier 2, then most students should be succeeding. But there will inevitably be a number of students who enter each school year lacking the foundational skills they need to learn at high levels. The five universal skills of learning include the following.

1.  Decode and comprehend grade-level text.

2.  Write effectively.

3.  Apply number sense.

4.  Comprehend the English language (or the school's primary language).

5.  Consistently demonstrate social and academic behaviors.

These skills are much more than a student needing help in a specific learning standard, but instead represent a series of skills that enable a student to comprehend instruction, access information, demonstrate understanding, and behave appropriately in a school setting. If a student is significantly behind in just one universal skill, he or she will struggle in virtually every grade level, course, and subject—and usually a school's students who are most at risk are behind in more than one area. So for students who need intensive remediation in foundational skills, the school must have a plan to provide this level of assistance, *without denying these students access to essential disciplinary outcomes*. This is the purpose of Tier 3 (figure 4.2). Because students develop universal skills over time, schools must provide intensive interventions for targeted students as part of their instructional day and by highly trained staff in the students' targeted areas of need.

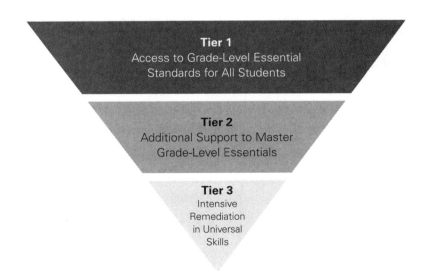

**Figure 4.2:** Tiers 1, 2, and 3 of RTI.

Last, and most important, some students are going to need all three tiers to demonstrate proficiency of the essential disciplinary outcomes at high levels—this is why it is called a multitiered system of supports. Students do not move from tier to tier. Instead, the tiers are cumulative. All students need effective initial teaching on essential disciplinary outcomes at Tier 1. In addition to Tier 1, some students will need additional time and support in meeting essential disciplinary outcomes at Tier 2. And in addition to Tier 1 and Tier 2, some students will need intensive help in learning essential outcomes from previous years. Students in need of Tier 3 intensive help in remedial skills will most likely struggle with new essential grade-level outcomes the first time they are taught. This means these students will need Tier 2 and Tier 3, all without missing new essential instruction at Tier 1.

An individual teacher in his or her own classroom cannot create this level of support, as the concept of the one-room schoolhouse shows. Instead, it requires a schoolwide, collective, collaborative, coordinated, all-hands-on-deck mentality. This is why structuring a school to function as a PLC is the key to effectively implementing RTI and ensuring that all students master essential disciplinary outcomes.

The RTI system of interventions ensures students master learning outcomes so schools can become highly effective, but how can schools emphasize progressive learning and promote student agency in relation to disciplinary outcomes? In the following section, we discuss this challenge.

# Four Ways to Challenge Students While Providing Student Agency

We have identified four practical ways to provide additional challenge to students with essential disciplinary learning outcomes.

1. **Voice and choice:** Provide the freedom to more deeply explore an area of student interest within the current content set to extend student learning.

2. **Depth and complexity:** Provide the option to explore more complex concepts within the existing content set to extend student learning.

3. **Interdisciplinary connections:** Explore a concept or idea across multiple disciplines to extend student learning.

4. **Real-world connections:** Provide a real-world context for the learning of the existing content set to extend student learning.

PLCs can implement all these strategies with varying degrees of student agency. Giving students ownership of question 4 demands careful consideration and planning.

We advocate strongly that this release be done carefully and in collaboration with the collaborative team. The teacher's role is to equip students to own their learning.

By using these strategies in isolation or combination, educators can teach students to challenge themselves beyond the assessed curriculum and ignite a passion for lifelong learning.

## Voice and Choice

The strategy of voice and choice uses personal interest to engage and challenge students. By providing voice and choice, teachers allow students to take control of their learning journey and explore a particular area of interest within the scope of the unit of instruction. To implement voice and choice well, it is important that teachers ask students to reflect on their learning and identify specific areas of interest. Frequently, the term *voice and choice* implies little structure or a free-for-all learning environment. To the contrary, PLCs must implement voice and choice intentionally and gradually in alignment with students' ability to self-monitor their learning. At the outset, using voice and choice should involve a highly structured, teacher-supported process. As students grow in autonomy, they are empowered to engage in this reflection with the teacher serving as a mentor. With voice and choice fully implemented, the teacher's role shifts to thought partner, as students take initiative and full ownership of their extension. Regardless of students' levels, the teacher plays an integral part in ensuring that student learning is focused and intentional.

## Depth and Complexity

Depth and complexity is the idea that students will have the opportunity to explore the content more deeply and with greater complexity through the exploration of differentiated materials. This strategy is widely applicable and one of the easiest to implement due to the opportunity for the teacher to serve as the initial provider of the additional resources. At the outset, the teacher commits to providing students a variety of resources from within the learning to explore. The resources then scaffold in complexity to allow students to choose their challenge. The next level of agency allows the students to mine a specific collection of resources to deepen their understanding and identify more complex ideas. With depth and complexity fully implemented, the teacher empowers students to dig into the content and discover more complex ideas without the support of teacher-curated resources.

## Interdisciplinary Connections

Interdisciplinary connections challenge students to broaden their understanding by looking at similar concepts via multiple subject lenses. In many schools, teachers supply this level of challenge by intentionally combining subjects, such as English and history, into a humanities course. In this context, students extend their learning by identifying the connections of the specific subject curricula to other subjects. To scaffold extension, teachers can begin by providing multiple connections for students to the current content. We recommend that the initial connections come from within the discipline, such as history to economics or chemistry to biology. The next level of extension would ask students to connect across disciplines such as science and art. We recommend that at the beginning, teachers provide the possible connections and the resources. As the students' skills grow in making connections, teachers can increase autonomy by simply providing possible lines of inquiry without resources. Ultimately, when schools allow the student to fully drive the extension, they ask the student to identify both the interdisciplinary connection and the additional material to explore the connection.

## Real-World Connections

Real-world connections of learning inspire students through the realization that what they learn in the classroom has practical applications. We find that there is no greater way to inspire students than to empower them to explore how academic content fits into the world. Unfortunately, all too often the level of learning delineated in the standards does not take students to a point of rigor where they apply their learning. By extending students through real-world connections, students gain a deeper understanding of the topic, and their motivation increases as they see the relevance of their learning. As with the other three extension strategies, the teacher should scaffold implementation. At the outset, the teacher can provide scaffolds by offering points of application with supporting resources. This allows the learner to see the application, yet explore it independently. The next level of autonomy could be to challenge the learner to identify the points of application from a prescribed list of possibilities. Full implementation could include allowing students to explore possible applications in their own life and identify resources that support the application of the content in the manner they identified.

The implementation of student agency for the fourth critical question allows the teacher to gradually release students on a path of inquiry while still ensuring they are within the traditional teacher-led classroom context. As students internalize extensions, they begin to independently deepen and extend their learning beyond the essential disciplinary learning outcomes. For this to happen, the teacher role begins to shift from leading learning to mentoring or coaching within the area of transdisciplinary learning outcomes. We explore such a co-constructed learning approach with transdisciplinary outcomes in the following chapter.

## Rate Your Progression

What collaborative systems and structures are in place in your school to ensure that all students learn essential disciplinary learning outcomes at high levels? What strategies have you used or would you use to release responsibility of critical question 4 of a PLC to your students?

## Tips for Transformation

The following are four tips to transform school culture.

1. **Build the learning experience:** Guaranteeing essential disciplinary learning outcomes requires the disciplinary collaborative team to be the architects of the learning experience.

2. **Adopt a teacher-led learning approach:** A teacher-led learning approach is the best approach for disciplinary learning outcomes—outcomes students must master.

3. **Ask and answer the questions:** The disciplinary learning outcome collaborative team is responsible for asking and answering the four critical questions of the PLC.

4. **Allow student agency:** A teacher-led learning approach allows students agency over their own learning as teachers release question 4, What will I do when I have already learned it? to students.

## Questions to Consider

Consider the following four questions as you begin your transformation to a highly effective and learning-progressive school.

1. **The learning:** What are the important learnings for me in this chapter? For my school? What am I inspired to know and be able to do?

2. **The evidence:** What are we already doing that aligns with this paradigm? What would change in my school and professional experience if we further embrace and implement it?

3. **The learning pit:** What obstacles would we face if we were to try or to further this approach? What strategies could we use to experience breakthroughs?

4. **The lever:** What would we need to accelerate the change process?

# 5

# Co-Constructed Learning for Transdisciplinary Learning Outcomes

In a co-constructed learning model, sometimes called a *co-constructed learning approach*, students and teachers share the responsibility for learning. The defining characteristic of this model is the acquisition of both the essential skills and dispositions to become an independent lifelong learner. With this model, teachers have higher expectations for learners as they develop autonomy and agency. During co-constructed learning, students continue to develop disciplinary knowledge, which expands to include the development of essential transdisciplinary skills and student-agency behaviors, sometimes referred to as dispositions. The collaborative team also considers how to begin to release agency to learners to allow degrees of personalization.

Co-constructed learning is built on the solid foundation of disciplinary learning in the guaranteed and viable curriculum, which is a hallmark of effective PLCs. The depth and breadth of student knowledge must increase to facilitate more complex integration of transdisciplinary learning outcomes. In the co-constructed learning approach, the disciplinary collaborative team is the group closest to students and remains responsible for delivering instruction. As teams progress in incorporating transdisciplinary learning outcomes, the disciplinary learning outcomes become the vehicle to demonstrate the transdisciplinary skills and agency behaviors. In essence, students demonstrate their disciplinary learning through the application of transdisciplinary skills in a personalized learning project.

In this chapter, we describe two components of transdisciplinary learning outcomes, the role of the teacher in ensuring mastery, the role of collaborative teams, and student agency using the four critical questions of a PLC.

# Two Components of Transdisciplinary Learning Outcomes

There are two vital components of transdisciplinary outcomes that work in tandem to build student agency: (1) transdisciplinary skills and (2) transdisciplinary dispositions. Students must have both the skills to learn and the dispositions to engage. These two outcomes require unique strategies. *Skills* are how to do something, and teachers can model, teach, and assess them. *Dispositions* are more discreet as they are founded in belief systems and require cultivation and reflection, and they are more difficult to measure. For example, we can glean from the research, such as from the Partnership for 21st Century Learning (Lai, DiCerbo, & Foltz, 2017), what skills are necessary to effectively collaborate. We can devise rubrics to measure collaborative skills and provide specific feedback to students on how to become a better collaborator. However, how do we measure a student's belief that collaboration is worthwhile and will result in a better outcome? A student may have the social skills to collaborate, but without the desire to collaborate, his or her skills are useless. Therefore, it is vital that schools focus not only on the skills-based outcomes, but also on the dispositions that allow students to apply their skills and engage in learning. We know these two outcomes are tethered—as students grow in skill, they also grow in disposition, and vice versa—yet we feel it is important to address each outcome discretely.

## Transdisciplinary Skills

As we have noted previously, transdisciplinary skills are often known as 21st century skills or future-ready skills. We refer to these skills as essential transdisciplinary skills as they support learning in all disciplines. We have intentionally not named a specific skills framework for essential transdisciplinary skills; however, as noted in chapter 1, there are multiple frameworks already available in the literature. We suggest that the best approach to identifying your essential transdisciplinary skills is to build from a proven, research-based framework. Common examples of essential transdisciplinary skills are critical-thinking skills, creativity skills, collaboration skills, and technology skills. The distinguishing characteristic of these skills is that teachers measure them through tasks that require their application.

## Transdisciplinary Dispositions

Transdisciplinary dispositions are much more challenging to measure as they are embedded in the core beliefs, values, and attitudes that drive student behavior. For a student to take ownership of his or her learning and gain agency, he or she must possess essential transdisciplinary dispositions. As with transdisciplinary skills, we do not prescribe a specific set of dispositions as the research is abundant with models; however, we strongly recommend (as we noted in chapter 1) that the model you choose include the following three ideas that strongly link with student agency: (1) self-efficacy, (2) grit, and (3) growth mindset. (We discuss these ideas in depth in chapter 1, page 19.)

During co-constructed learning, teachers explicitly model and teach essential transdisciplinary skills while they cultivate dispositions through the manner in which they engage students. Both are vitally important to empower learners with agency.

The key to incorporating transdisciplinary learning outcomes into instruction is challenging students to move beyond surface-level disciplinary knowledge and into deep, complex learning using transfer tasks that allow students to drive the learning process.

With a co-constructed learning approach, it is even more vital to clearly articulate the guaranteed and viable curriculum. Just as disciplinary content builds over time, so does the mastery of transdisciplinary skills and dispositions, across multiple grade levels. While it is possible to implement a co-constructed learning approach at a specific grade level or in a particular classroom, we strongly recommend a systematic, schoolwide approach for long-term sustainable student agency. In our experience, when schools take a systematic, multigrade approach, students grow in confidence and agency as they internalize their learning process and are able to autonomously apply the skills required for deep and transfer-level learning.

## Role of the Teacher in Ensuring Mastery

For students to master transdisciplinary learning outcomes, the teacher's role shifts from being the expert to being the learning coach. In the learning coach role, the goal is no longer driving the learning at the whole-class level; instead, the teacher begins to tailor the learning process for each student. Learning evolves into a more small-group, microteaching format, and ultimately implementation of individualized conferencing strategies. In a co-constructed learning environment, students take on additional responsibility for their learning over time as they develop their transdisciplinary skills and agency behaviors. The teacher serves as the lead learner and learning coach, consulting with students and modeling learning expertise.

In this approach, collaborative teams of teachers still accept full responsibility for learning, but they expect the learner to embrace his or her role in the learning process. In the co-constructed learning approach, classroom teachers no longer use differentiated strategies; they provide a menu of teacher-modeled strategies for students to access in their learning process to personalize the learning. As the expert learner, the teacher supports the learner to apply a variety of strategies to attain the essential disciplinary and transdisciplinary learning outcomes. The teacher's primary role in a co-constructed learning approach is providing an authentic, strategy-rich, and visible learning environment that supports student agency.

For students to thrive in a co-constructed environment, the teacher must create a learning laboratory where students have access to the essential tools to own their learning journey, such as:

- Clear learning outcome expectations

- Articulated proficiency bands with clear criteria between bands

- Exemplar work in each proficiency band

- A robust strategy bank appropriate for the learning

- A growth mindset environment that celebrates failure, reflection, and iteration

- Learning outcomes that enable students to personalize their learning, such as a common entry point, but an open-ended exit point

With the incorporation of the transdisciplinary learning outcomes within the guaranteed and viable curriculum, learning how to learn becomes the most important element of a co-constructed learning approach. The disciplinary learning outcomes become the medium from which the transdisciplinary learning outcomes build. Thus, the teacher's identity must shift from being the most knowledgeable in a discipline to being the expert learner.

## Collaborative Teams in a Co-Constructed Learning Environment

As we discussed in chapter 3, collaborative teams in PLCs are made up of educators who share essential learning outcomes for their students. The co-constructed learning model needs two teams with specific team structures and time for collaboration. The primary work continues to evolve around the disciplinary outcomes team—the typical type of team in a PLC—the grade-level team in primary school or the common course team in secondary school. The second collaborative team is the transdisciplinary outcomes team. This team's role is to create a systematic and progressive skills curriculum that is *life-worthy*, one that prepares students with the future-ready skills to meet the expected schoolwide learning results, or what Jay McTighe and Greg Curtis (2015) refer to as *impacts*. McTighe and Curtis (2015) define impacts as desired student learning outcomes that represent the aspirations of a school's vision and the core of its mission. These learning outcomes, or impacts, are long term and performance oriented, require transfer, and are performed with autonomy.

## Disciplinary Outcomes Team

The disciplinary outcomes team is responsible for learning and instruction. They continue to be the point of interaction with students. The team's core work is still on creating common tools for instruction focused on the essential learning. The team creates clear learning targets, identifies proficiency criteria, and plans common assessments and proficiency criteria; however, now the lens for this work is the development of student agency by using the disciplinary learning to facilitate transdisciplinary skills. As with a teacher-led approach, the disciplinary team's organization is most often by grade level or common course.

## Transdisciplinary Outcomes Collaborative Team

The role of the transdisciplinary outcomes team is to identify the scope and sequence for the skills and dispositions that will be applicable and transferable to all learning—the future-ready, transdisciplinary skills. As we mentioned in chapter 1, schools can choose from a variety of models and formats for these skills. The specific outcomes that each school selects should match its mission and core values, and also align with its curriculum long-term transfer goals. We believe teams must consider the following three criteria when developing the transdisciplinary outcomes.

1. The outcomes must transfer to all disciplines.

2. The outcomes must be future focused and real-world relevant.

3. The outcomes must be age-appropriate across the grade continuum.

The transdisciplinary team's work is to identify the outcomes, clearly articulate them in a coherent scope and sequence, and establish proficiency criteria for each grade level or band. Many schools that have effectively implemented transdisciplinary skills have done so in grade bands as opposed to grade levels. Using grade bands, the school is respecting the developmental progressions of individual students, yet clearly communicating proficiency targets for students and teachers. The best scope and sequence work we have seen has also included a level of specificity that creates a coherence of experiences for students that allows for transfer of skills and dispositions between classrooms and grade levels. These scopes and sequences can include the following.

- Strategies to cultivate student growth mindset, self-efficacy, and agency

- A common language of learning

- Student assessment and reflection strategies

- Suggested metacognitive strategies

The degree to which the team articulates strategies depends on each school; however, we have learned that transfer of agency behaviors occurs most effectively when the approach across the school is consistent and common.

## Team Structures and Time for Collaboration

A co-constructed learning approach requires the disciplinary outcomes team to commit to a more intense and focused collaboration. In our experience, schools have approached this collaborative work in different ways depending on where they are in the continuum of becoming a highly effective and learning-progressive school. In schools that are just starting to incorporate essential transdisciplinary outcomes, the transdisciplinary teams generally work as supplemental teams operating outside of the school's disciplinary teams. The supplemental teams consist of educators divided into teams that focus on the identification and articulation of specific transdisciplinary outcomes. The supplemental teams initiate the work by identifying the essential transdisciplinary outcomes and then develop a transdisciplinary skills scope and sequence. The strategies for approaching this work can vary. For example, in larger school systems, we have seen the transdisciplinary teams take the shape of a district task force that then refers the transdisciplinary scope and sequence to district disciplinary teams. In smaller independent schools, this process is often whole school. The most important thing, as McTighe and Curtis (2015) note, is that the transdisciplinary learning outcomes, or impacts, are long term and performance oriented, require transfer, and are performed with autonomy. These clear transdisciplinary outcomes then provide the necessary foundation to guide the disciplinary collaborative teams as they design instruction.

Once the team identifies and articulates the essential transdisciplinary outcomes, the schools we observed incorporated more time in two distinct ways, often progressively, to create the space for collaboration around skills and behaviors.

1. Initially, many schools simply carve out additional protected meeting time for disciplinary collaborative teams to incorporate the transdisciplinary skills into their scope and sequence. This time can take on many forms. We have seen schools utilize full-release days, early-release and late-start times, and professional learning days. Time is a precious commodity, and the amount of time teams have to collaborate will influence their rate of progress.

2. Once the curriculum is clear and the teams embed transdisciplinary outcomes into the guaranteed and viable curriculum, teams begin to evolve into more real-time collaboration that takes place on an ongoing basis beyond the weekly team meeting with the goal of incorporating students into the collaboration.

For many schools, traditional structures are hard to abandon. It is not uncommon for schools to leverage their existing structures and carve out more time for disciplinary collaborative teams to meet. Schools use the structures that have traditionally worked in their context, usually for more content-focused collaboration, and transfer them to collaboration for skills and behaviors. In one school we visited, the disciplinary team met on Monday and Thursday with a flexible focused agenda that incorporated essential knowledge, transdisciplinary skills, and learning behaviors. In this structure, teachers still worked fairly autonomously during instruction but closely collaborated on the learning outcomes. The biggest long-term limiting factor to this structure is the inability to incorporate the student into the conversations as the school evolves to incorporate personalized learning.

As schools progress in empowering students with agency, they realize that the student is key to collaboration. We have seen collaboration evolve into more real-time, student-centered collaboration in which schools still gave disciplinary collaborative teams a protected time to meet; however, schools often combined classes and teachers co-taught and gave students moderated feedback in real time. In these schools, much of the collaboration around student-agency behaviors and transdisciplinary skills involves the students and teachers engaging in structured dialogue about student evidence of learning. Feedback and reflection with students become part of instruction, which mitigates the need to have additional structured meeting time. Disciplinary teams that progress to this point are approaching a personalized learning approach in their collaborative practices (we discuss this approach further in the next chapter).

# Student Agency in a Co-Constructed Learning Approach

In a co-constructed learning approach, student agency ranges from initiating to nearly autonomous, as learners span a continuum in their acquisition of transdisciplinary skills and dispositions. This range of difference among students requires a highly differentiated approach to instruction that allows the learner to take more leadership of his or her learning as he or she progresses in agency. In a co-constructed learning approach (as in the teacher-led learning approach), teams and teachers ask and answer the four critical questions of a PLC, and they gradually release these questions to students as they develop agency. As in teacher-led learning, teachers release the fourth question—How will we extend the learning for students who are already proficient?—to students, with the ultimate goal of then releasing critical questions 2 and 3 to learners as they progress in autonomy.

## Critical Question 1

In a co-constructed learning approach, ownership of question 1 still belongs to the teachers and the disciplinary collaborative team. However, it is important to note that the work of the disciplinary team evolves based on the transdisciplinary outcomes team's work. This is apparent in the development of a coherent language of learning that shifts away from teacher-focused language, moving to more student-centered language. The change in the learning language frames the disciplinary learning goals to incorporate transdisciplinary learning outcomes into the co-constructed learning approach. To review, table 5.1 shows examples of the shift in language and focus for the four questions.

TABLE 5.1: Teacher-Focused Versus Student-Focused Language for the Four Critical Questions

| Teacher-Focused Language | Student-Focused Language |
| --- | --- |
| 1. What do *we* want students to know and be able to do? | 1. What do *I* want to learn and be able to do? |
| 2. How will *we* know students have learned it and are able to do it? | 2. What evidence will *I* provide to demonstrate that *I* have learned it? |
| 3. How will *we* respond if students do not learn it or are not able to do it? | 3. What strategies will *I* use if *I* get stuck or am not making progress in my learning? |
| 4. How will *we* respond if students are already proficient to deepen their learning? | 4. What strategies will *I* use to deepen or personalize my learning? |

Shifting the four questions to student-focused language allows students to connect with the disciplinary learning outcomes while building transdisciplinary skills and dispositions. It is vital that the learning targets and curriculum are accessible to students to support agency and student ownership.

## Critical Question 2

Since the focus of a co-constructed learning approach is to build students' transdisciplinary skills and dispositions, we believe that after releasing question 4, the next logical question to release to students in the learning process is question 2, How will we know if they learn it? Part of the disciplinary outcome collaborative team process is clear articulation of the learning targets for knowledge, skills, and dispositions. Proficiency criteria and progressions must accompany the learning targets. With these clearly articulated, releasing question 2 becomes a natural extension of instruction and a key vehicle for growing agency.

Releasing question 2 requires a shift in the focus around assessment. By incorporating both disciplinary and transdisciplinary outcomes into the guaranteed and viable curriculum, the assessment tasks that teachers present to students become more sophisticated and complex. The collaborative team must move away from rigid, disciplinary-focused common assessments and focus on the development of tasks that present a common entry point but allow the learner to determine the exit point. The common assessments must focus on transfer and incorporate the transdisciplinary and disciplinary skills. As such, the assessment tasks do not have one right answer, but provide multiple answers, allowing the learner agency in assessment. Although there are multiple answers, tasks should be based on the clearly articulated common proficiency criteria. This shift is key to giving agency to the learner, but equally important is the collaborative team's ability to continue to use learning data to ensure high levels of learning for all students. In embracing this new paradigm for common assessment, collaborative teams are able to incorporate assessment strategies that provide agency such as student self-assessment, reflection, goal setting, action planning, and progress monitoring as part of core instruction. These skills are essential for growing student agency and autonomy in learning.

Teams can release assessment at an early age—we argue the earlier the better. We have traditionally conditioned students to be extrinsically motivated by achievement. Stakeholders have viewed the teacher as the evaluator and giver of marks. By releasing assessment to students, we shift their paradigm from achievement to learning. The teacher is no longer the evaluator as the student takes a greater role in providing evidence of learning that meets these specific criteria of the standards.

Equally important, teachers must shift their beliefs of their role in assessment. Teachers are no longer the guardians of grades, nor are they in the business of sorting students into achievement bands. By empowering students to own their assessment, educators shift to an orientation that a student's demonstration of learning can take on a variety of forms and still remain valid. This is a particularly difficult philosophy to embrace with older students. In our experience, secondary teachers struggle with this philosophy shift much more than elementary school teachers. By empowering students with assessment, teachers must accept that validity lies in assessment criteria, not in the sameness of tasks or equality of actual evidence students provide.

When moving toward student-driven assessment, we recommend that you incrementally implement the following three layered approaches.

1. **Personalize the mode:** By allowing students to personalize their mode of assessment, students take ownership of the demonstration of learning.

2. **Use evidence-based assessment:** Often called portfolio-based assessment, students provide evidence and reflect on their learning by target.

3. **Personalize the pace:** By allowing students to self-pace their learning and assessment, you provide flexibility and support.

## Personalizing the Mode

Allowing students to personalize the mode of assessment is an easy first step in providing students ownership of assessment. While standards and objectives often dictate the level of rigor a student must demonstrate, offering choice in the assessment task allows students the ability to match assessment with their preferred learning style. Choice in assessment begins to create an environment that cultivates dispositional outcomes. Instead of experiencing an assessment the teacher is *giving* the student, the student has the power to *engage* in demonstrating his or her learning on a task of his or her choice. While subtle, this shift changes mindset and efficacy. As a scaffold for initial implementation, we recommend the teacher provide choice during an assessment. By controlling the choices, the teacher is providing more autonomy but still ensuring the assessment's validity. Additional release would allow students a choice of mode based on their personal preferences without teacher restriction as long as the mode of assessment allows students to demonstrate the necessary rigor, standards, and learning outcomes.

## Using Evidence-Based Assessment

The next level of personalization is evidence-based assessment. Evidence-based assessment empowers the learner to curate his or her evidence of learning based on his or her personal learning progression. Evidence-based assessment fully empowers learners to create a portfolio of evidence that they feel meets the learning targets and proficiency bands. Evidence-based assessment places the student in the role of curator and evaluator. The teacher then takes on the role of learning coach, providing feedback and confirming the student's findings. The final mark is then an agreement between the student and teacher on where the evidence the student provides fits within the assessment criteria. Evidence-based assessment gives the student the choice of assessment mode and pace. In addition, it allows the student to continuously reflect on evidence in relation to the assessment criteria and revise his or her work.

## Personalizing the Pace

Allowing students to personalize the pace is the final progression in allowing students to own question 2. A core understanding in PLCs is that all students can learn, though students learn at different rates and in different ways. Teachers must differentiate time and curriculum to ensure all students learn at high levels. By allowing students to choose the pace and possibly the sequence in which they assess, we are ensuring that students have flexible time and support.

Often the biggest limiter of our ability to allow students to choose the pace of assessment is the holdover of an industrial model of age-based grouping. Teachers must consider how they will accommodate for students pacing at different rates as they develop units. Teachers must be prepared to deepen learning for those who demonstrate mastery quickly, and support students who are progressing slowly. It is important to note that *deeper* does not mean *different* learning—just more depth to the learning. One of the most effective strategies for deepening learning is to transfer agency to students and make the learning transdisciplinary.

## Critical Question 3

As students' transdisciplinary skills and dispositions grow, teachers in highly effective and learning-progressive schools begin to release question 3. Students begin to ask themselves, "What will I do when I am not learning?" Students reflect on their learning and identify where they may need some additional time and support. In releasing question 3, the teacher expects students to partner with him or her in identifying the reasons they may be struggling with a particular learning target. The expectation of advocacy leads to student ownership of the learning. It also facilitates student buy-in and willingness to accept the necessary support to achieve. The teacher, as the lead learner, is a key resource to facilitate student intervention. The teacher's level of involvement can range dramatically based on a student's ability to reflect and revise, yet regardless of the student's level of autonomy, the teacher is still the one ensuring that the student is progressing toward proficiency.

Empowering students to be active in their intervention plan is a tiered process and heavily dependent on how well developed the learner's student-agency behaviors have become. We observed that the following four items allow for students to drive their intervention.

1. **Metacognition:** Students reflect on and understand the way they learn and the processes that support their personal cognition.

2. **Self-assessment:** Students understand the learning expectations and are able to identify the gaps between their work and proficiency.

3. **Support planning:** Students are able to devise a plan of support that accelerates their learning and specifically addresses their learning gaps.

4. **Learning partners and tools:** Students have identified learning partners and tools for support that help them in the journey toward proficiency.

The teacher is a key component to supporting students in acquiring the skills and dispositions to diagnose their learning gaps. The teacher serves as a learning mentor and coach in helping students engage in the reflective cycle it requires to build a student-directed learning intervention plan. We have seen these strategies effectively implemented with students across the age continuum. At its core, the process stays the same. What varies is the use of developmentally appropriate strategies, such as pictures in early childhood education, graphic organizers in elementary school, and reflective questioning in secondary school.

## Metacognition

*Metacognition* is a student's ability to understand how he or she learns best and what learning strategies will help him or her become an efficient and effective learner. No two students learn in exactly the same way. Students who understand their brain and how to learn efficiently with their unique set of talents are at a distinct advantage. The teacher's role during the intervention cycle is to offer various options to support the learner in identifying strategies that are particularly effective for his or her personal learning challenge. For instance, if a student is struggling with organization and task completion, common metacognitive supports would include setting goals, planning work, chunking assignments, and creating checklists. If a student is struggling with reflection and evaluation, common supports include reflective question guides, anchor examples, comparison charts, and next-step examples. Fluency in metacognition allows students to diagnose their learning challenges. For students to have agency during intervention, they must understand what strategies work for them and which do not.

## Self-Assessment

If students are to have agency in intervention, they must be able to identify their learning gaps and the next steps in the learning process. Core to self-assessment is the ability of students to engage in a reflective cycle in which they ask themselves the following three questions, which take critical question 3 of a PLC to a deeper level.

1. How does my work stack up against these criteria?

2. What, if any, are the areas in which my work needs improvement?

3. Where do I need additional time and support to meet proficiency?

Students' ability to reflect and self-assess has been shown repeatedly to have a dramatic effect on achievement (Hattie, 2008). There is no age requirement for engaging in this practice. The younger students begin to engage in this process, the more they internalize ownership of the learning process. The teacher's role in this intervention process is to provide feedback, but more importantly, to help students reflect on their evidence of learning against these criteria to self-diagnose areas in need of improvement. The teacher's role as learning coach and mentor is critical in ensuring students are mastering outcomes as they build a sense of ownership and self-awareness. We have seen this strategy used beautifully across all grades. At Stonefields School, we observed early learning students comparing their work to pictorial exemplars posted in the room and then revising their work. At Shanghai American School, secondary students were provided checklist criteria along with reference exemplars for quality and were required to authenticate their learning with a peer. The reflection and self-correction in action were remarkable.

## Support Planning

Developing a plan of support has traditionally been the teacher's role. We believe that for students to own their intervention, they must have the power to develop a systematic plan of support for their learning. In our experience, when students understand themselves as learners and have the ability to reflect on their performance, they also understand what they need to do next to grow. Yet often, educators take control of a student's plan and impose a specific set of actions that the student must do to meet expectations when he or she gets behind. We fully respect and admire teachers' desire to actively participate in creating, supporting, and monitoring the student's plan of support. The teacher's role in the intervention processes is critical; however, our goal is for the student to grow in agency. As a reminder, we define agency as the student's ability to take specific and purposeful action to impact his or her level of success. There is no greater place for students to demonstrate agency than in their ability to develop, implement, and reflect on a support plan. In our experience, when teachers have control of the interventions, students are often engaging in compliance instead of learning. In a shift from compliance to ownership, teachers transition the ownership of the plan to the students, while continuing to monitor the plan's progress. Taking the role of the learning coach allows teachers to actively engage students to ensure they progress while empowering them to take action and progress in learning.

The student-driven support plan looks different for various levels. In early childhood, we have seen students engaged in a reflective conversation with the teacher and offered options of support. In upper elementary, we have observed students engaged in learning journals that ask them to document challenges and note when they feel challenged or frustrated and then engage in a conference with a teacher to evaluate the challenge and brainstorm solutions. In secondary school, the array of strategies expands. We have seen students empowered with the opportunity to lead team meetings and create success journals that document when the strategies they are using succeed and then how to transfer that success to areas of challenge. What is important in the support planning is not the specific strategies in use, but rather student engagement in the process. In engaging the student, teachers normalize struggle as a productive part of learning, as opposed to a barrier to success.

### Learning Partners and Tools

For students to own their intervention plan, they must also know they are surrounded by partners who will guide them if they get stuck. Ownership does not mean isolation. Students must know the resources they have at their disposal to support their learning plan. Each school has a unique set of supports that can range dramatically. Once students know how they learn, where they are faltering, and what their plan is, they must know what resources they have at their disposal to support their plan.

Allowing students to drive their own intervention plan is a challenge for many teachers and schools. This is the reason we suggest release of question 3 later in the continuum of release. We fully acknowledge that, at times, the teacher must take ownership of the intervention plan. In addition, while the intervention we describe focuses specifically on learning or skill issues, often learning issues arise due to social-emotional or behavioral factors, or *will* issues. Whether skill or will, it is vital that students understand what is causing their learning gaps and how to take action to improve their situation. We have observed during our work that often teachers must take a more active role in working with students on will issues. Students who are skill deficient are more often able and willing to own their plan than students who have will deficits. Intuitively, this makes sense to educators, for students who are struggling with emotional issues, instability at home, or life challenges often disengage from school. In these circumstances, teachers must take a more assertive approach to support students and seek the support of the school intervention team as part of the RTI process. Even when a student is facing such challenges, it is important to engage him or her openly and expect the student to participate in the process.

## Critical Question 4

As with the teacher-led learning approach, the easiest place to start for students in releasing responsibility with the co-constructed learning model is to release critical question 4, What will I do when I have already learned it? How will I extend my learning? What do I learn next? once students demonstrate content proficiency on common assessments and begin to demonstrate the essential transdisciplinary skills and agency behaviors. Releasing question 4 (described in chapter 4) allows students to practice their newly discovered agency behaviors and apply their new skills. The strategies for releasing question 4 are the same as those for teacher-led learning, covered in chapter 4.

The sophistication of student skills and behaviors dictates the depth to which teachers release the question.

# Autonomy Versus Support

The co-constructed learning approach is potentially the most complicated and complex period for both learners and teachers. The line between autonomy and support is fine and highly individualized to the learner. Additionally, each learner will progress at a different rate, and, thus, the levels of agency and autonomy will vary greatly from student to student. In moving your students to a co-constructed learning approach to learning, it is important to identify the continuum that differentiates the teacher-led learning approach and the co-constructed learning approach in terms of student agency (see table 5.2).

TABLE 5.2: Student Agency in Teacher-Led Learning Versus Co-Constructed Learning

| Construct | Teacher-Led Learning Approach | Co-Constructed Learning Approach |
|---|---|---|
| **Collective Responsibility** | Teacher teams take collective responsibility for student learning. | Students partner with teacher teams to take collective ownership and responsibility for learning. |
| **Curriculum and Learning Targets** | The school district and teachers own the guaranteed and viable curriculum. | Teachers and schools own the guaranteed and viable curriculum. The curriculum expands to include transdisciplinary skills and student-agency behaviors. Students understand, partner in the development of, and can articulate their learning targets, which now include knowledge, skills, and behaviors. |
| **Formative and Summative Assessments** | Teachers design, administer, and evaluate common formative and summative assessments. | Teachers design common formative and summative assessment tools. Teachers partner with students to provide feedback and facilitate reflection. |
| **Learning Data** | Teachers analyze formative and summative learning data. | Students and teachers analyze and make meaning of the formative and summative learning data. |
| **Interventions** | Teachers design interventions for students when they are not learning. | Students partner with teachers to develop a personal intervention plan with strategies to empower students to own their growth. |
| **Extensions** | Some students receive extension once they demonstrate they can access grade-level expectations. | Students receive opportunities to personalize learning as part of initial instruction. |

## Rate Your Progression

Co-constructing learning requires a strategic approach to change that initially leverages the areas within the school, team, or curriculum that are most likely to succeed. What are the areas in your learning community where you would be able to initiate a co-constructed learning approach? What would be your initial action steps to get started?

## Tips for Transformation

The following are four tips to transform school culture.

1. **Chunk the shift:** There is no one right place to start when developing a co-constructed learning approach. We advise collaborative teams to chunk implementation and initially focus on the transdisciplinary skills and dispositions that most easily integrate with the existing disciplinary outcomes. We also advise teams to make the skills and dispositions transparent to learners so they are aware of the shift you are asking them to make.

2. **Focus on authentic agency:** When developing the co-constructed learning approach, be sure to focus on the definition of agency and find places where students can take authentic ownership of their learning. Students will know if you are still in control. You must provide a meaningful first experience so students build efficacy and agency.

3. **Embrace the ambiguity:** Expect that both teachers and students will be uncomfortable. Teachers are used to being in control, and students are used to being led to the answer. Incorporating student agency is a paradigm shift for both the learner and teacher that takes time and sustained effort.

4. **Engage in self-compassion:** As educators, we feel tremendous responsibility to ensure our students learn. Giving them the proverbial keys to the kingdom is going to feel awkward at the outset. At times you will feel like you are losing control and want to take it back. In these moments, it is natural to assert yourself more in the learning process. Don't feel bad; just realize what is happening and find the right time to increase agency. This process is a push and pull. It will take time to get to personalization.

**?**

## Questions to Consider

Consider the following four questions as you begin your transformation to a highly effective and learning-progressive school.

1. **The learning:** What are the important learnings for me in this chapter? For my school? What am I inspired to know and be able to do?

2. **The evidence:** What are we already doing that aligns with this paradigm? What would change in my school and professional experience if we further embrace and implement it?

3. **The learning pit:** What obstacles would we face if we were to try or to further this approach? What strategies could we use to experience breakthroughs?

4. **The lever:** What would we need to accelerate the change process?

# 6

# Personalized Learning

One of our school visits took us to the plains of Middle America: Cedar Rapids, Iowa. We listened in to the following conversation between two science students.

> **Student 1:** "We need to figure out how to focus the laser so the receptor can pick it up at twenty to twenty-five feet. I think we need to look at including a new lens that can direct and columnize the beam."
>
> **Student 2:** "If you look at the beam at 1 inch and then 1 foot, we are losing a lot of focus. Our budget constraints for this project are under one dollar, so we need to come up with an innovative solution."
>
> **Student 1:** "Mr. J., could we borrow you for a minute? Because we have some questions about ray theory."

This is a typical dialogue between students and teachers at Iowa BIG. BIG's goal is to personalize learning around meaningful community-based projects. The school uses a *scrum* approach to teaching and learning that puts the students at the heart of the learning process. The students choose a community-based initiative, or design their own, and engage a team of students in solving the problem. The teachers serve as learning mentors, project coaches, and confidants. At BIG, students choose the projects, and the school matches the standards. Visit BIG for ten minutes, and you immediately see the power of agency and personalization.

As we see in this example, personalized learning moves students to the center of the learning process. It challenges the traditional structures of school, moving away from old classroom structures and knowledge transmission in favor of a student-directed, resource-rich learning hub model in which tools of learning are accessible and students select which ones to utilize at which point in time to make the most progress. Students learn in an environment in which the school empowers them to make the necessary learning moves to advance their progress, personalizing their pathway.

In the personalized learning approach, learners take full ownership of the learning. Students ask and answer all four of the PLC critical questions from their perspective. As a result, students determine how they learn and at what pace they learn.

For students to take control of their learning, highly effective and learning-progressive schools devise new constructs for organization. We identify three key organizational shifts that schools must make.

1. **From traditional classrooms to learning hubs:** In order for students to drive their learning, they must have access to the tools of learning, including teachers, specialists, learning resources, technology, and so on. When schools desire personalized learning as the outcome, they must shift from classrooms to learning hubs.

2. **From lockstep curriculum to personalized pathways:** As the guaranteed and viable curriculum focuses more on skills and becomes content agnostic, students can determine what they want to learn and in what manner they want to learn it. They personalize their learning with a pathway of their choosing.

3. **From a set pace to personalized progressions:** Students who personalize their learning progress through the curriculum at their own pace. Learning becomes a continuous, personalized cycle of inquiry. Progression ebbs and flows as students engage in more challenging tasks.

# Learning Hubs

For schools to become learning progressive, they must evolve their organizational structures that support learning, such as the facilities, the attendance policies, and the master schedule, to allow for the flexibility needed to personalize learning. We recommend learning hubs, which advocate a central location for all learning tools. A learning hub unites teachers into a common space to facilitate student learning. In the learning hub, teachers' collective responsibility for learning is active and visible. Students can collaborate with multiple teachers about their pathway and progression. The learning hub team works together to group and regroup students based on interests, learning styles, necessary interventions, and where students are in their learning progression. Specialists, ranging from librarians, technologists, language-support personnel, research specialists, and so on, move into and out of the learning hub as needed to support learners.

In a learning hub, teachers can efficiently and effectively work collaboratively as they empower students to ask and answer the four critical PLC questions for themselves. In this common space, students meet, study, receive guidance and feedback, conference with teachers and specialists, and engage in instruction as they need to. The beauty of the learning hub is that it shifts the orientation from students moving around the school to the school moving around the students. The shift facilitates real-time collaboration and conferencing with students as part of the work of collaborative teams. Many schools have evolved spaces simply by taking out a common wall and replacing it with a movable partition, but this is the challenge: How do we evolve physical space to actually reflect the needs of learners? Many schools we visited have successfully made this transition.

# Personalized Pathways

Personalization through pathways can take many forms. Some schools chunk personalization and structure it as a specific part of the school day, while others make an intentional effort to build their entire program around choice of pathways. The choice of how to personalize pathways is often subject to a school's specific local context, such as physical location, community support, school structure, transportation, and so on, and might include structured time or programs and courses.

## Structured Time

For many schools, the first step to student agency is to provide structured time for student choice. Highly effective and learning-progressive schools incorporate time for students to engage in self-determined learning. During these blocks of time for learning, students develop learning plans, often to explore interests that frequently take on the form of projects. Typically, these structured pathways are extensions of learning that connect to the curriculum in some manner. The structured time is meant for cultivating skills and dispositions of learning, thus often specific content is not the focus. Schools use standards to prescribe the specific content students need to learn; however, the specific resources and materials that students use to learn the standards can be almost entirely up to the student. We found that highly effective and learning-progressive schools incorporate this structured time into the program's core, giving students agency to pursue their interests and passions by asking and answering the four critical PLC questions for themselves.

In one elementary school we visited, students were provided with 20/20 time; each day they had twenty minutes to work on their agency project, and every twenty days they received the full day to work on their project. The school chose the 20/20 moniker as it also intimated to parents that it was the child's vision of learning coming to life. In a secondary school we visited, students were provided every tenth day of school to work on a transdisciplinary, student-developed project supervised by a learning mentor. In yet another school, every grade level culminated with a four-week agency unit where students could deepen their understanding of a topic in the curriculum and transfer their learning to address a community challenge. The format of the structured time can vary; however, it is vital that students are given enough time to fully meet the curricular expectations.

## Programs and Courses

Teachers and schools further along in the personalized learning journey moved beyond designated time to incorporate personalization into all aspects of their programs or courses. Students in these schools and classrooms have agency to drive their own learning. Even though the degree of choice varies, student choice exists in virtually every aspect of the learning journey. Students have choice over the core aspects of learning that are traditionally left to teachers: content, experience, and assessment. The following are just a few examples to illustrate how some highly effective, learning-progressive schools and teachers are empowering students to own their learning journey. We provide additional, in-depth examples of how to personalize learning for different grade levels in real schools in chapter 7 (page 107), chapter 8 (page 125), and chapter 9 (page 145).

In one school we visited that embraced the concept of initiative-based learning, students identified a problem in their community they wanted to solve, developed an initiative to resolve it, and then partnered with their teachers to identify the learning they required to complete the initiative. They identified how their plan fit into the various essential disciplinary learning outcomes and developed a course for credit. The teacher was available to support the students in their learning and to determine if each student had met the curricular expectations. Within an initiative-based learning environment, the teacher guards the guaranteed and viable curriculum, yet the student is the architect of his or her learning.

At Shanghai American School, teachers structured entire units and courses around student agency within particular curricular expectations. The teachers created unit learning logs that clearly communicated what essential transdisciplinary learning outcomes students must demonstrate to be proficient and a single-point rubric to anchor proficiency expectations. The teachers then created an exhaustive list of resources and learning activities that aligned to specific learning targets that students could choose from to engage in learning the material. The teachers created shared online learning and assessment calendars that became the contract between the students and the teachers of the unit or course. Students could then customize the calendars to create their personal learning and assessment plan. Students then followed their personal calendar, utilized the resources to engage in the activities as they chose, and took assessments as scheduled. Additionally, students often identified their own learning resources and developed their own activities to deepen their learning. The most progressive teachers also abandoned the traditional forms of assessments and used the products of the learning activities as evidence of learning. These teachers used additional strategies such as conferencing, reflection, and portfolios as evidence of learning.

## Personalized Progressions

In our experience, personalized learning requires schools to abandon the traditional industrial model, or set pace, of curriculum. For students to be empowered with personalized progressions, schools must be high-functioning PLCs, and teachers must already embrace the many aspects of personalized learning. Personalizing progressions empowers students to move their agency beyond the content and materials. Students no longer progress through school at a common pace. Instead, they advance through the established learning progression (curricular scope and sequence) at their own pace with clearly delineated personal learning outcomes that include identified success criteria and learning benchmarks they create in partnership with the teacher. The student drives the learning and uses learning hub resources to support his or her learning. The teacher team is present to ensure that the student progresses and meets his or her personal learning goals and to guard the guaranteed and viable curriculum. Equally important, while learning progressions allow students to learn the curriculum at their own pace, there is a reality that students will need to progress at a rate that prepares them to successfully transition to post-secondary no later than the end of grade 12. This means teacher teams must monitor student progress to ensure every student is on track to achieve this goal. As students learn, they provide evidence for teacher validation that they have attained goals, and then they progress to their next learning outcome.

Personalized progressions allow students to use their areas of interest to obtain and demonstrate proficiency of the guaranteed and viable curriculum at their own pace with a specific focus on their needs. Students accelerate in areas in which they have strength and receive support in areas that challenge them. A fundamental tenet of PLCs is to ensure high levels of achievement by making time and curriculum the variables and achievement the constant. Personalizing progressions allows us to live this maxim for every student in all content areas through the personalization of time and curriculum. Essentially, students and teachers partner as a collaborative team to create a personalized experience for each learner.

The construct of personalized progressions fundamentally challenges the cohort-based, grade-based industrial education system—the set pace. Thus, many existing schools cannot identify the structures to move to personalized education where pathways and progressions drive learning.

We have visited a number of schools that have attempted to create personalized learning environments. It is important to note that many of them have not yet achieved being both highly effective and learning progressive. The few schools that are both highly effective and learning progressive were built around the core concepts of PLCs and invented themselves or reinvented themselves as personalized learning organizations, allowing them to shed some of the traditional barriers to implementation. We outline such a daring change process in chapter 10 (page 169). One such traditional barrier is the shift in the role of teacher from learning coach to learning mentor.

# Role of the Teacher in a Personalized Learning Approach

A personalized learning approach requires the teacher to move from learning coach to learning mentor. Teachers regularly consult with each individual learner to provide inspiration, advice, feedback, and validation. The teacher ensures each student has a sound pathway that meets the learning agreements and helps connect the student with resources that will advance his or her learning. The teacher serves in a reflective capacity for the student, using the skills of an expert learner to ask questions and prompt student thinking to propel students to higher levels of learning. When the student is ready, the teacher takes the role of authenticator, using the proficiency criteria to provide feedback and validate the student's work. The cycle of learning continues until all students have attained their agreed-on goals.

It may seem like personalized learning diminishes the teacher's role as content expert. We agree that the role of teacher as content purveyor greatly recedes. However, as students reach greater content depth and fluency, the role of the teacher is even more vital in the personalized learning approach. Students work on a variety of disciplinary content at various paces and from individualized perspectives. The breadth and depth of student learning are greater in a personalized learning approach, and as a result, teachers must have broader and deeper content knowledge to support student inquiry. In schools that function predominantly in a personalized learning approach, the most common challenge for faculty is the shift created as students explore topics that even teachers are not familiar with. This produces a co-learning environment in which the teacher becomes the learning partner, using his or her expert learning skills to support students. Coincidentally, in the schools we visited, it is in these moments when teachers serve as learning partners that teachers reported feeling most inspired and instrumental to the students' progress.

It is important to note that at different times in the learning cycle, the teacher's role will change to match the students' needs. If the student shows signs of trouble, the teacher will need to coach. If the student is clearly off track, the teacher will use a teacher-led approach to get the student back on track. The collaborative team continues to be responsible for student learning, and should monitor and adjust its teaching approaches as needed.

## Collaborative Teams in a Personalized Learning Approach

Collaboration is at the heart of professional growth and development in a personalized learning environment. It provides the single best opportunity for teachers to perfect their craft, through "collective inquiry and action research" (DuFour et al., 2016) about student learning. Working in collaborative teams is quite simply the best way to become a better teacher, particularly as the teacher's role continues to evolve (DuFour et al., 2016).

In personalized learning, the work of the disciplinary and transdisciplinary collaborative teams continues to occur simultaneously as established in a co-constructed learning approach. However, the core of collaboration will continue to focus on the disciplinary team. The core work of the disciplinary team in personalized learning focuses on creating the tools to facilitate student agency while still holding to the three big ideas of a PLC.

PLC collaborative teams have frequently been composed of teachers who share a common curricular outcome, such as in grade-level or course-alike teams. We expect that collaborative teams continue to be those educators who share common curricular outcomes; however, as schools increase their focus on transfer of tasks and transdisciplinary outcomes, the teams are organized by the students they serve in the learning hub and are made up of educators from diverse disciplines. In personalized learning, the transdisciplinary outcomes become the ends, and the disciplinary outcomes are the means. In personalized learning, only the student and learning mentor (teacher) are consistently part of the collaborative team. The collaborative team is created for the learning at that moment with a variety of disciplines present. The disciplinary team may include peers, other teachers from the same discipline, transdisciplinary teachers, support teachers, specialist teachers, real-life experts, and so on. As the learning progression changes, disciplinary team composition will change as well. The collaborative teams are no longer fixed. The disciplinary team changes and evolves as the students' learning focus changes.

In the teacher-led and co-constructed learning approaches, teachers continue to take the collective responsibility for ensuring high levels of learning for all students. In a personalized learning approach, teacher teams share the collective responsibility for learning with students. Students gain the ability to drive their learning and take full ownership of all four PLC questions. While the teachers retain copilot status in ensuring learning, the students become the captain of their learning journey. This revision of collective responsibility requires a change in the roles and structures of teachers and learners in framing and answering the four questions. Teachers and students share the process for answering the four PLC questions with both groups having integral roles in ensuring learning at high levels.

While collaborative teams in teacher-led and co-constructed learning approaches schedule protected time for teacher teams to collaborate around the four critical questions of a PLC, the personalized learning approach requires schools to move beyond scheduled collaborative time and incorporate real-time collaboration with the students as part of instruction. Since students in a personalized learning environment are increasingly empowered to personalize their learning pathways and learning progressions by asking and answering the PLC questions for themselves, and teacher teams are facilitating a continual cycle of inquiry based on the needs and progress of each student, learning hubs create a seamless collaborative environment with students learning alongside teachers in collaboration. Collaboration takes on a distinct orientation: structured and in real time. The disciplinary collaborative team will still have a structured and protected time for collaboration; however, the focus of this structured time is primarily on critical questions 1 and 2. In a personalized learning approach, teachers must still utilize their professional expertise to translate disciplinary and transdisciplinary outcomes into a student-accessible language of learning. They must collectively create common learning targets to facilitate student ownership of critical question 1. In addition, the disciplinary team uses its structured time to create assessment tools. The team creates the common assessment criteria, identifies proficiency levels and the learning progressions relative to proficiency, and agrees on anchor exemplars of proficiency. Essentially, the team must still work to clearly articulate a common guaranteed and viable curriculum.

The work of the disciplinary collaborative team is even more important in a personalized learning environment in which learning targets are less concrete. It is impossible to guarantee that students have demonstrated mastery of transdisciplinary outcomes at the same level of proficiency in a self-directed manner unless teachers work with colleagues to clearly understand what mastery looks like for that particular skill. In a highly effective and learning-progressive environment, it is imperative for teachers to work together and come to a shared understanding of learning targets.

Once all members of the disciplinary team are clear about what students need to learn and have a clear vision of proficiency, the collaboration occurs in real time. The disciplinary collaborative team no longer waits for a weekly meeting to create learning plans, provide feedback, and respond to student work. In a learning hub model, these things happen as part of the process of daily learning. The teacher, working as a learning mentor, and other members of the disciplinary team consult with students to empower them to answer the four PLC questions. They support students in developing a learning plan to meet proficiency, self-assessing using the assessment tools, and prompting them to and helping them reflect and respond when they get stuck, and they help inspire students to deepen their learning through personalization.

# Student Agency in a Personalized Learning Approach

The release of student agency in a personalized learning approach begins with the release of critical question 1 (content)—a distinction from the other approaches, which begin with the release of question 4—and continues with questions 2 (evidence of learning), 3 (intervention), and 4 (extension).

## Releasing Question 1 in a Personalized Learning Approach—Content

The release of question 1—What do I want to know, understand, and be able to do?—is the most challenging, so we reserve it for the highest learning level, personalized learning. Researchers (DuFour & Marzano, 2011; Wiggins & McTighe, 2007) clearly articulate that an essential component to high levels of learning is a guaranteed and viable curriculum for all students.

As we discussed with teacher-led learning, the guaranteed and viable curriculum most frequently comes from a set of learning standards and requires interpretation from expert teachers. While we acknowledge the teacher's importance in clearly translating the standards into a student-friendly and accessible curriculum, a personalized learning approach requires teachers to involve and empower students to curate the curriculum in a personalized manner that inspires and engages them. In some disciplines, especially in those that are largely skills focused, the opportunities for curriculum personalization are vast. In disciplines that have highly content-focused or sequentially focused curriculum, the opportunities for personalizing the curriculum are more constrained. Yet regardless of curriculum, some personalization is possible.

A common misunderstanding with personalized learning is that there is no core content and each student will learn different material. We hope that by now we have made it clear that the guaranteed and viable curriculum is non-negotiable; students must still master the essential disciplinary learning outcomes. What changes with personalization is the student's ability to impact the context of his or her learning. For example, students are no longer doing the same mathematics problems, but they are learning the same mathematics outcomes. They are no longer completing the same laboratory experiment, but they must all demonstrate specific laboratory skills. This is the reason we have intentionally selected personalization versus individualization. Personalization empowers students to demonstrate proficiency by the curricular expectations in their own pathway and progression, but the expectations are still systemic and consistent. Individualization customizes the learning targets to the strengths and weaknesses of each student with a common outcome being differential expectations.

There are numerous strategies for offering personalization of the curriculum to students. We combine them into the following three distinct categories.

1. **Student-friendly curriculum:** The curriculum is in age-appropriate language that allows the students to interpret and interact with the learning.

2. **Content in the skills curriculum:** Students select the content when the focus of the curriculum is skills based.

3. **Curriculum bundle and sequence:** The curriculum is flexible, and the school empowers the students to bundle and sequence the learning.

We fully recognize that there is a continuum of ownership of the curriculum that directly correlates to student age; however, all students, at minimum, should have the power of knowing what they are going to learn.

## Student-Friendly Curriculum

Student agency in curriculum begins with students having a clear understanding of the learning outcomes. Framing the outcomes in student-friendly, age-appropriate language allows the students to understand what they are going to learn and to what degree they are going to learn it. In our experience, the best teachers at communicating learning in a student-friendly manner are early childhood teachers. Elementary teachers, often due to the age of their students, are very explicit in communicating what students are going to learn, why they need to learn it, and what the criteria are for proficiency. As students age, what was previously made explicit is often expressed implicitly, leading to unnecessary miscommunication and lack of clarity.

Step one in empowering students to drive the curriculum is ensuring they have a clear understanding of the following.

- The specific learning outcomes for the unit

- The criterion for proficiency for each learning outcome

- The overarching concepts the unit targets, often referred to as enduring understandings and essential questions

After clearly articulating the curriculum, the next step of release is providing choice of content in the domains of skill.

### Content in the Skills Curriculum

More and more, learning standards are focusing more on skill development and less on content. For example, the National Council for the Social Studies (2013) *The College, Career, and Civic Life (C3) Framework for Social Studies State Standards* is virtually content agnostic; students can choose from a variety of historical content to learn the heavily skills-based curriculum. Many subjects, from art to music to literature, have specific skills that students can learn using a variety of materials. These are high-leverage areas schools can use to empower students to take ownership of the curriculum by offering more choice in the what and how of learning. Take for example the Common Core English language arts standards, which are almost exclusively skills focused. These standards provide high leverage for students to choose the medium, text type, and assessment mode so long as they demonstrate the skill.

### Curriculum Bundle and Sequence

Schools often reserve bundled or sequenced curriculum for the oldest and most mature students. Allowing students to bundle and sequence the curriculum gives them the ability to define how they will learn. In essence, we are saying, "This is what you have to learn; how do you want to learn it?" This open-ended approach to curriculum offers students the autonomy to drive their learning with remarkable depth. In doing so, students gain a level of understanding and engagement that they rarely accomplish with teacher-controlled curriculum.

There are several important scaffolds to consider when engaging in this level of release. First, it is easiest to release to this depth when the curriculum is largely skills based. For example, the Common Core English language arts standards are heavily skills based with virtually no specific reference to content. In this environment, students may demonstrate learning through a variety of means, making it ideal for release. Second, in a course that can be taught in multiple ways, the teacher may offer multiple possibilities to group or sequence learning. For example, a history course can be taught thematically or chronologically. Allowing the class to choose which orientation is an additional scaffold. Finally, the teacher is still responsible for ensuring students engage in the guaranteed and viable curriculum, so mentoring and coaching are integral to ensuring students engage deeply in the right learning.

## Releasing Question 2 in a Personalized Learning Approach—Evidence of Learning

The creation of common formative assessments, looking at the evidence of learning and student feedback, is a critical part of the PLC process. Critical question 2 for students asks them to consider, "How will I demonstrate that I have learned it?" One of the greatest challenges with a teacher-led learning approach is the pacing of learning. Teachers teach each unit at approximately the same pace so that the collaborative team members can administer formative assessments at approximately the same time, analyze the results together, and give students useful and timely feedback to help them move toward mastery. This cycle is one of the most powerful processes for improving student learning.

In a personalized learning approach, common assessments no longer mean giving the *same* assessment. As schools give students voice as to *how* they will demonstrate their learning, students also have the opportunity to choose *when* they will demonstrate mastery of essential learning outcomes. In a highly personalized learning environment, students are held to common assessment criteria applied to student evidence of learning. The commonality is found in the learning criteria, rather than in the assessment itself. The common criteria allow teacher teams to use evidence of student learning to reflect on the effectiveness of both individual teachers and the team instructional practices.

With personalized learning, learning is the constant, and time is truly the variable. Since students are responsible for their learning, they have the opportunity to accelerate through the curriculum or slow down based on their mastery. As a result, teacher feedback on evidence, especially formative evidence, is immediate and relevant to a student's personalized learning plan. Students and teachers are part of the collaborative team that co-constructs student assessments.

## Releasing Question 3 in a Personalized Learning Approach—Interventions

One of the most challenging teaching skills is differentiation. In a teacher-led learning approach, the best teachers develop this artful skill over years of faithful practice. But even the most-gifted teachers are only able to differentiate instruction and interventions to a limited degree. By empowering students with agency, teachers using personalized learning are able to better differentiate to each individual student's needs. In a more traditional structure, this is simply impossible.

A personalized learning approach creates structures that empower students to identify and select intervention strategies that work for them to answer critical question 3, "What will I do when I am not learning?" It should never be an option for students to choose not to learn the essential learning outcomes, but they should receive a lot of choice when it comes to how they choose to learn them. In a personalized learning approach, students continue to apply the strategies they learned during the co-constructed learning approach; however, they must have the opportunity to have complete agency of their learning plan, even when they are not learning. When students are stuck, they have to rely on transdisciplinary skills and agency behaviors to get unstuck. Students continue to have access to collaboration with the disciplinary team; however, it is the student's responsibility to engage in collaboration with his or her team, his or her learning mentor, and the resources of the learning hub.

When the student is not making adequate progress in the progression, the learning mentor first engages the student in a reflective process to develop a personal intervention plan. This plan takes stock of what he or she has attempted, and strategizes how the learner could use additional learning tools at his or her disposal. The learning mentor and student co-create the personal intervention plan that the student then initiates. If during the next check-in the student still hasn't progressed, the learning mentor intervenes and takes more ownership of the personal intervention plan to support the student. The pattern of more directed intervention continues until the student makes the necessary progress.

It is important to note that even at this high level of personalization, the teacher or learning mentor is still responsible for ensuring students learn at a high level. If at any point in time a student falls significantly behind the curricular expectations, the teacher would take on more responsibility in ensuring the student progresses. The further behind the student is, the more responsibility the learning mentor takes. Once the student is making satisfactory progress, agency is released back to the learner. In our experience, once learners have agency, they crave it, and their motivation increases, thus it is our belief that if a student falls significantly behind, he or she requires adult intervention.

## Releasing Question 4 in a Personalized Learning Approach—Extensions

A personalized learning approach creates opportunities for students to go beyond the curriculum and pursue their areas of interest and passion. With teacher-led learning, schools accomplish this through differentiation in the regular classroom, where each student who demonstrates mastery of the intended learning targets receives time to explore the concept deeper and further or design a project that allows him or her to apply the learning in new ways.

In personalized learning, teachers create time in the schedule for extension opportunities when students explore their interests and passions by asking and answering critical question 4 entirely for themselves: What will I do when I have already learned it? The depth and sophistication of students' experience lies entirely with them. If they progress quickly, they can choose to go deeper or accelerate their learning with a specific pathway or progression. The learning outcomes for these opportunities can vary greatly; what is important is that students are in control of the learning process. Chapters 7 through 9 explore real examples of schools that are providing time for students to ask and answer question 4 at every grade level.

# Ownership of the Four Critical Questions

To become a highly effective and learning-progressive school, you need to consistently focus on personalized learning. Students must have ownership of all four questions, be supported by a teacher acting as a learning coach, and be able to control their pathways and progressions, as table 6.1 shows. It is important to realize that all schools, even those that are highly effective and learning progressive, are at various levels at different moments in time. No school, not even all the schools we visited, uses a personalized learning approach all the time. Sometimes it is necessary to use a co-constructed learning approach if there are gaps in knowledge or skill present, or even a teacher-led approach if students lack skills to access proficiency. Additionally, it is plausible that you could have students accessing different approaches within the same learning space. Yet regardless of the circumstances or the students, highly effective and learning-progressive schools should strive to use personalized learning approaches with their students. We believe involving parents as partners in personalized learning is a key to success.

TABLE 6.1: Student-Agency Comparison—Co-Constructed Learning Versus Personalized Learning

| Construct | Co-Constructed Learning | Personalized Learning |
|---|---|---|
| Collective Responsibility | Students partner with teacher teams to take collective ownership and responsibility for learning. | Ownership for learning shifts to the students as they become members of the collaborative team. |
| Curriculum and Learning Targets | Teachers and schools own the guaranteed and viable curriculum. The curriculum expands to include transdisciplinary skills and student-agency behaviors. Students understand, partner in the development of, and can articulate their learning targets, which now include knowledge, skills, and behaviors. | Students take ownership of the curriculum and curate the curriculum to meet their interests and needs. Teachers translate the standards into student-friendly language that allows students to personalize the curriculum. |
| Formative and Summative Assessments | Teachers design common formative and summative assessment tools. Teachers partner with students to provide feedback and facilitate reflection. | Teachers design common assessment tools. Students use these tools to inform their personalized learning plan and goals. Students use these tools as progress markers to their goals and for reflection. Teachers use these tools to validate student evidence and confirm students attain the learning goals. |
| Learning Data | Students and teachers analyze and make meaning of the formative and summative learning data. | Students submit evidence of learning to demonstrate proficiency. Teachers collaborate with students to provide critique, feedback, validation, and reflection. They use data to inform learner best practices and inform how learners could learn differently in the future. |
| Interventions | Students partner with teachers to develop a personal intervention plan with strategies to empower students to own their growth. | Students seek support when they get stuck. Students access a network of support tools and develop a personal intervention plan in partnership with the teacher and support tools. |
| Extensions | Students receive opportunities to personalize learning as part of initial instruction. | Students engage in deeper exploration of their learning within the cycle of personalization. |

# Parents and Personalized Learning

Effective parent partnerships enhance learning. As schools move to a more personalized approach, it is vital that they educate parents throughout the transition. Remember that most parents experienced the traditional industrial model of education. They understand the comparison-based, sort-and-select system and all the institutional legacies that come with it, such as letter grades, percentages, tests, and so on. It is for this reason that we believe schools must first become an excellent and effective PLC before moving to become progressive with personalized learning. Parents want to know what their child is expected to learn, how learning will be measured, and what support their child will receive if he or she struggles, and they want an assurance he or she will be challenged—all addressed by the four critical questions of a PLC. All parents know their child is unique; we have found that parents are very supportive when schools honor their child's unique interests and talents.

As schools move along their personalized learning journey, it is essential to remember to take the time to empower parents as much as students. Schools should consider the following three actions to empower parents to partner in their student's learning.

1. **Connect parents to the learning goals:** Whether the teachers create curricular goals or students personalize them, parents should have access to these learning goals.

2. **Show the process of learning:** As much as possible, make the student's learning process visible. Online portfolios, microblogging platforms, and paper portfolios all provide access to the learning process and allow parents to see student progress.

3. **Show them the evidence:** Nothing is more powerful for demonstrating learning than the physical products of learning. Schools have always relied on summary reports, such as report cards, to show learning. We recommend that you show parents their student's work, in conjunction with feedback and reflection. Some schools even go as far as having the parent reflect on the work against the goals and criteria.

We have found in our work, and in the schools we visited, that if parents know what their child is expected to know, can see their child's progress, and ultimately see their child achieve the expectation, they are content and supportive.

### Rate Your Progression

Personalization of learning is a challenging shift as it requires a fundamental restructuring of school as most educators have experienced it. What are the structural shifts you must consider to facilitate agency and personalization?

## Tips for Transformation

The following are five tips to transform school culture.

1.  **Remember it takes a village:** The personalized learning approach is dynamic and fluid. Success largely will depend on the willingness of the educators to collaborate with students in real time in a multidisciplinary environment. The collaborative team must be responsive and flexible, with educators revolving around the students as the need arises.

2.  **Choose pathway *or* progression:** Many people take on too much when starting with personalization. Remember to first teach the skills and dispositions students require to have agency. This is most easily done through a shift in pathway. Once you are confident students can lead their learning, then initiate choice in progression.

3.  **Map the journey:** Educators have found it useful to create a visual that maps students by their place on the scope and sequence of transdisciplinary outcomes since students progress differently in their ability to take ownership of their learning. Mapping the students' transdisciplinary skills allows educators to predict when and where students might struggle and make sure teachers are available to provide support as needed.

4.  **Empower parents:** The personalization shift is often alarming to parents. It is best to over-communicate with parents and share learning plans you are creating with students so that parents can support their children at home. Parent workshops that empower parents with the right reflective questions can help students share their learning journey at home.

5.  **Learning is the constant:** While the aim is to personalize, it is important to remember that sometimes students require direct intervention. Giving students agency does not free teachers of the responsibility that all students should learn at high levels. When needed, intervene, support, and then return agency.

## Questions to Consider

Consider the following four questions as you begin your transformation to a highly effective and learning-progressive school.

1. **The learning:** What are the important learnings for me in this chapter? For my school? What am I inspired to know and be able to do?

2. **The evidence:** What are we already doing that aligns with this paradigm? What would change in my school and professional experience if we further embrace and implement it?

3. **The learning pit:** What obstacles would we face if we were to try or to further this approach? What strategies could we use to experience breakthroughs?

4. **The lever:** What would we need to accelerate the change process?

# PART THREE

# Putting Theory Into Practice

# 7

# From Theory to Practice in Elementary Schools

In this chapter, we illustrate the personalized learning approach by sharing the stories of schools that are committed to offering programs that are progressive in design without sacrificing the high levels of learning for students. We hope that these examples from elementary schools will encourage you to try something new in your school.

At the heart these elementary schools is a desire to give students agency over their own learning process. You will see examples of how elementary schools are empowering students to ask and answer the four critical questions of a PLC for themselves. While some schools do not explicitly use the four critical questions of a PLC, all of them have an inquiry process that fits nicely within the PLC framework.

First, we share the story of the Stonefields School.

## Stonefields School

The Stonefields School, on the outskirts of Auckland, New Zealand, is an unassuming public primary school with an extraordinary team of educators leading it. At the helm are educators like Sarah Martin, principal and Ollie Baker, deputy principal, passionate and articulate leaders who are empowering their truly diverse students to personalize their learning outcomes for their very economically and culturally diverse student population. This highly effective and learning-progressive school embodies the ideals and principles of personalized learning we lay out in this book. We observed both personalized learning pathway and personalized learning-progression in this school. Rarely have we seen students more able to articulate where they are in the learning process and in their learning progression than at Stonefields—a rich environment for student voice. We begin our look at Stonefields with a description of its staff members' collaborative efforts and how students ask and answer the four critical questions of a PLC. The section ends with a story from grade 4 student Natasha in her own voice.

## Collaboration

Collaboration is a vital component of learning and teaching in the 21st century, and it is one of four vision statements at Stonefields. The school's physical space lends itself to collaboration. Three teachers staff each learning hub, and each hub is the size of three traditional classrooms. The school assigns learners a guardian teacher for administrative purposes, but learners do not remain in these home groups for the duration of their day. Learners work with different teachers in the hub depending on the subject area they are studying and other factors, such as skill level and relationships. Students might see one teacher in a hub for a numeracy clinic on fractions and proportions, and another for a writing follow-up session and use of complex sentences. This allows for strength-based teaching and facilitates relationship development between teachers and learners since students are not locked into having a single teacher for the duration of the year.

Both teachers and students are learners and teachers at Stonefields; the mind frame that learners need to wait for the teacher to espouse knowledge is almost nonexistent. Learners are encouraged to collaborate with teachers and other learners to develop their knowledge in a content area. For example, if Stonefields doesn't offer numeracy clinics on a given day, then it empowers learners to work with another learner in the class who can assist with the delivery of the same information. It is not uncommon to see students sharing their understanding with each other, testing each other's level of proficiency, and working on creative collaborative projects.

*Smart collaboration*—the ability to decide when it is pertinent to work together and when it is not—is a vital skill that teachers actively model and teach to their learners at Stonefields. The school also promotes awareness for when and where to seek feedback. The open-door policy fosters the seeking out of knowledge and ideas, beyond a traditional teacher-student relationship.

Hub teachers plan with one another, calibrate their understanding of learning-target proficiency, construct projects, and develop interventions when learners are not learning. They share their work instantly with the entire school staff (and the world) on their grade-level websites.

There can be tension when determining when to choose collaboration and when to work alone, and teacher actions are on display in the learning hub for all to see. While this can mean an unmasking of self-imposed personal shortcomings and "weaknesses" as a teacher, the opportunity for growth is phenomenal. If teachers are truly dedicated to having all students learn at high levels, then teachers must be just as open to learning as they insist their learners must be.

## Critical Question 1: What Do I Want to Know, Understand, and Be Able to Do?

The program at Stonefields allows learners to see their yearlong learning journey in its entirety and to identify all of their own learning goals for the day. All students at Stonefields are responsible for the pace of their learning progressions. The school has aligned the learning progressions to the New Zealand national curriculum, following students from grade K to grade 8. Students have learning progressions in the core curriculum areas of reading, writing, and numeracy, but also for their learner qualities and graduate profile, they have a set of dispositions and skills that the school has identified as essential for success. These learning progressions ensure that students clearly understand what they must know and be able to do according to the national curriculum, while giving them almost complete autonomy as to how and when they demonstrate mastery of the standards. Learners highlight where they think they are in their learning and then consult with their teachers to make sure they have correctly placed themselves on the progression.

The school uses a digital platform to track and monitor the learners' placement on each progression, so learners (through self-monitoring), teachers, and parents have anytime access to the learning progressions. Learning is a continuous self-directed and personalized process.

With the learning progression, learners see their current learning focus, what they have previously focused on, and what their next steps are. Because their progressions stay with them the entire time they are at Stonefields, they are able to keep a record of their learning. This helps teachers design learning that is relevant for each student.

As one student at Stonefields said to us, "I like to think of the progressions as a really detailed road map for my learning. They let me see what's come before, where I'm standing now, and as far as the eye can see . . . and more."

## Critical Question 2: How Will I Demonstrate That I Have Learned It?

Each of the learning standards the learning progression articulates has an "add evidence" option that allows learners to upload evidence for each learning target. This is how learners show that they have understood the learning.

Learners have the ability to get creative as they demonstrate mastery of very clear standards. Students seem to fully engage in this strategy because it lets them communicate their learning on their own terms and look at problems in multiple ways. Learners can upload multiple pieces of evidence to any progression, from a spelling focus in writing to an exponent number strategy in numeracy. Evidence of learning can transmit in any format—via a document, a website link, or a video, for example. As one can imagine, some learners have some really creative ways of demonstrating mastery, including by creating movies, documentaries, and dances, all to showcase their learning.

The teacher conferences with the learner and analyzes the evidence of progression. The learner is then free to move on to the next standard. The evidence of learning stays on the progression so that if a learner gets stuck, or forgets a strategy, he or she can go back and look at the learning for that progression.

## Critical Question 3: What Will I Do When I Am Not Learning?

At Stonefields, getting stuck in learning is very much part of the learning process. In fact, students celebrate being in *the pit*. It is a great place to be since teachers, learners, and parents understand it to be a necessary challenge to take learning to the next level. The program deliberately equips learners with the tools necessary to get themselves out of the pit. To own their learning process, learners must use these tools available and their strategies when they are not getting it.

Digital tools give learners the ability to access potential collaborators to help get out of the pit. Students collaborate with teachers, local and global experts, and their friends. Google for Education apps, and the staggering amount of content creation and sharing programs available online, allow all learners to access information instantly, with feedback being almost immediate and highly visible. With this proliferation of possible feedback opportunities, it is becoming even more vital that learners and teachers are able to select appropriate feedback to give, and determine whether they are the optimal people to do so. Stonefields learners are taught to be self-aware in the feedback they give and to whom they give it to maximize their learning.

## Critical Question 4: What Will I Do When I Have Already Learned It?

Stonefields has embraced a concept it calls *breakthrough time*, originally modeled after Google's 20 percent rule that gives employees 20 percent of their time to pursue their own creative work. Today, Stonefields learners spend up to 40 percent of their time (two full days a week) exploring their areas of passion and interest. This time, which is entirely student driven, has had a significant positive impact on the school's culture. Evidence of student engagement and learning at high levels can be seen everywhere you look.

Beyond breakthrough time, Stonefields created an extra learning opportunity program, or ELO, in which learners deliver minilessons to another individual or small group within the hub. The reciprocal learning and teaching can be highly effective, but teachers must ensure that the learner delivering the ELO has the necessary content knowledge and collaboration skills to do so. At Stonefields, the effective delivery of an ELO is a sign of sound understanding or mastery in an area. ELOs are not limited to just the core learning areas of reading, writing, and mathematics. This collaborative teaching approach is hugely beneficial, as it allows learners to show mastery in varied fields, from fly-fishing to crocheting to rocket building. See Student Voice: Stonefields School to learn one student's experience.

### Student Voice: Stonefields School

My name is Natasha. I am in grade 4 at Stonefields School. My day often begins with a focused look at my learning progressions on a map that shows the core learning areas of reading, writing, and mathematics that I need to learn. For example, today there is a literacy session that I will participate in with some of my friends. This is a clinic my teachers offer during the day. My learner progressions document what I have achieved so far, what my current learning goal is, and a clear progression for my next steps. These learning progressions start in grade 1 and end in grade 9. The great thing about Stonefields is that I can go as far as I can or as slowly as I need to go in order to learn everything.

Once I have looked at my progressions in literacy, I can make the choice if I need to attend the available workshops. This choice is based on my current step, but I may also choose to go if the clinic available is one of my future next steps, or an area that I am really interested in. If I don't go to the literacy session, I can use my learning time to construct evidence that I can map into my current learning progression. These tasks are not simply created to map a specific standard, but are whole tasks that I can carry out over a number of literacy sessions. As I get older, the tasks become longer. Our teachers help us to unpack the learning progressions, meaning to understand the different components of a writing or reading strategy and what this looks like in a learning task.

continued ➡

Numeracy learning is also based on my individual learning progression. The government in New Zealand makes sure that all students can do mathematics well, so this is really important. There are clinics for mathematics as well. We can use many different tools to create learning, including books, Google Docs, pictures, short movies, or recordings with learning apps, which all help us with the task at hand. If the school isn't offering clinics, then I can actively build my own knowledge using the model of the learning process. We are taught to find information that is relevant to our current goal. In this way, we are encouraged to not wait for a teacher for the answers. Since students outnumber teachers thirty to one, we could be waiting a long time!

For all learning areas, Stonefields encourages its students to provide an ELO where necessary. One student might help another learn a multiplication place value strategy or teach a clinic to illustrate when a learner should begin a new paragraph in his or her narrative writing. This builds on one of our philosophies at Stonefields—that we are all teachers and learners, a statement that my friends and I are quick to remind our teachers of.

# Singapore American School Elementary Spanish Program

The Singapore American School (SAS) elementary school Spanish program, led by teacher and elementary Spanish coordinator Cris Ewell, has implemented a proficiency-based model of program design and language instruction. This approach places students on a learning continuum based on their level of proficiency. The elementary Spanish collaborative team has worked hard to give students agency of their learning progression while holding students to very clear standards of mastery for their essential disciplinary learning outcomes. This is that program's story. We examine first how collaboration works in the program and then how students ask and answer the four critical questions of a PLC. Finally, the section wraps up with a story from a student.

## Collaboration

In order for teachers in the K–12 Spanish program at SAS to collaborate effectively, they must all work from the same understandings of a progression of interpersonal oral language proficiency based on the American Council on the Teaching of Foreign Languages (ACTFL) Assessment of Performance Toward Proficiency in Languages (AAPPL) measure descriptors. In this framework, SAS divides the levels of novice through advanced low into smaller steps. It breaks novice into N1, N2, N3, and N4, while intermediate is divided into I1, I2, I3, I4, and I5. SAS language teachers attend oral proficiency interview (OPI) training, which further defines the categories of novice and intermediate, but also gives a more complete definition of the advanced and superior levels of language competency.

SAS teachers receive common training, but it is also important to ensure that teachers have a common and practical understanding of proficiency levels from kindergarten to grade 12 and that students and the community at large have the same understanding. To begin this process in elementary school, SAS creates a spreadsheet in which its teachers list all students. Teachers conduct and record a small sample of student interviews. They discuss in teams the outcomes of the interviews and what needs to improve in the interview process to increase the probability of valid results. They then interview, record, and rate all students based on adapted rubrics from the AAPPL measure descriptors. Each teacher has a column in which to rate each student. In this way, teachers measure the reliability among all five teachers on the team. Once they establish reliability within the team, they share the spreadsheet and links with the middle and high school coordinators, asking them to select a random sample of students from the list and provide their perspectives about the student ratings. This conversation continues for several years and expands as students reach higher and higher levels of proficiency.

Every year, the language teachers administer the AAPPL test to measure the validity of their internal instrument. After OPI training, they also do a random selection of fourth- and fifth-grade students and record OPI-style interviews. They transcribe and analyze these data from these interviews and then compare the OPI ratings to the AAPPL ratings.

This level of personalized learning is not possible without creating a collaborative culture among teachers and students. Part of creating the common understanding among teachers around proficiency targets involves making the language simple enough for all students to understand them as well. Since the program begins in kindergarten, teachers must make the progressions simple enough for kindergarten students to grasp. One teacher began this process by creating a growth chart similar to that which students would have next to a door frame to measure their height. He kept the language very simple.

**N1:** Answer in a word.

**N2:** Answer with some words or phrases.

**N3:** Answer with memorized sentences.

**N4:** Answer with my own sentences.

Figure 7.1 shows a sample spreadsheet the team uses to ensure inter-rater reliability among teachers.

| Student | Recording | Teacher 1 | Teacher 2 | Teacher 3 | Teacher 4 | Teacher 5 | Middle School Team | High School Team |
|---------|-----------|-----------|-----------|-----------|-----------|-----------|--------------------|------------------|
| John | Interview link | N4 | I1 | N4 | N4 | N4 | N4 | I1 |
| Sally | Interview link | N3 | N4 | N3 | N3 | N4 | N3 | N4 |

N1 = Answer in a word; N2 = Answer with some words or phrases;
N3 = Answer with memorized sentences; N4 = Answer with my own sentences.

**Figure 7.1:** Sample spreadsheet to establish common ratings in student oral proficiency.

At first, teachers questioned whether the younger students would be able to grasp a proficiency rubric that had puzzled professionals for so long. The answer came from a student when two colleagues were sitting at a table eating with a first grader. They were speaking Spanish, and a first-grade student decided to join in.

"Do you like your food?" asked the student in Spanish.

One of the teachers, Rogelio Bolaños, looked at the little person across from him, slightly amused at his bid for conversation among the adults. "Yes," he answered, in Spanish.

The student looked at Mr. Bolaños very seriously and explained, "Señor Bolaños, if you don't use complete sentences, you're never going to get out of novice!"

Once students understand the proficiency progression, they learn how to rate themselves and to rate each other honestly in order to help one another grow. For a good example, consider students in an intermediate class who are able to identify when a student answers in one sentence, a list of sentences, connected sentences, or organized sentences. They have word lists that help them identify connected sentences and organized sentences and are able to give feedback to each other as to what is missing to get to the next level of proficiency. When students begin to approach intermediate high, they learn how to give different types of feedback in regard to grammatical errors. Students understand that it is not criticism; rather, the class is functioning as a big team. The goal is that everyone on the team reach high levels of proficiency. Students evaluate themselves and evaluate (or "help coach") each other as they practice for the teacher's evaluation, who uses the same rubric. Students get feedback from the teacher in regard to the progression so that they know exactly what they need to do to move to the next level.

## Critical Question 1: What Do I Want to Know, Understand, and Be Able to Do?

The Spanish collaborative team found that it cannot assume that everyone believes learning another language is valuable. The team has to be purposeful in showing students why and how learning another language is valuable in their lives. Once the team establishes this value, it focuses on the explicit use of rubrics to help students understand the guideposts in the path toward learning another language.

Students practice toward very specific *I can* statements in each class period that target a defined outcome. An example of a day's goal might be, "I can compare and contrast my life with the life of baseball player Roberto Clemente."

There is a scaffolded Venn diagram with common key words and structures at the front of the room. There is also the rubric of I1 to I4 so that students know what they need to achieve at each level. At the outset of the class, students write the goal of the day (in Spanish) and set their own personal proficiency goal (I1 to I4).

## Critical Question 2: How Will I Demonstrate That I Have Learned It?

Even though the class may have students at the levels N3, N4, I1, I2, and I3, students work in pairs with other students who have a difference of one to two degrees of proficiency, talking about Roberto Clemente's life and their own lives. Students then switch partners and retell the same story and ask questions. Finally, only the scaffolding of images (with no words) remains, and students retell the story to a third partner. The last five minutes of class, students record a quick video in which they record their story and put it on their blog as a means of demonstrating how they can talk about the target for the day. Before leaving, students reflect as to whether they met their proficiency goal for the day, and what they feel they need to achieve the desired level.

Another example of a means of demonstrating mastery is to have students create a play or present a collaborative work of art. The process by which students create the play shows as much (or even more) about their proficiency as does their final product. The need to negotiate meaning in order to complete a creative collaborative project of their choice brings an opportunity for the teacher to observe a lot of conversation and provide specific feedback. The practice toward a final presentation also raises awareness of new vocabulary and structures.

## Critical Question 3: What Will I Do When I Am Not Learning?

Since students have a clear understanding of what their learning targets are and can choose how they are going to demonstrate proficiency at each level, it is only natural that students advocate for themselves when they are not progressing in their learning. An example of student empowerment in a novice class is that teachers have different centers set up around the room, each one aiming for a different target. Students know for which targets they have demonstrated mastery, and on which targets they still need practice. They choose their centers based on what they need to learn. By choosing their own centers, students control their own learning and what they need to work on, even in the very limited linguistic environment of novice.

## Critical Question 4: What Will I Do When I Have Already Learned It?

Students receive rubrics that show not only their nearest progression target, but also the progression steps that go beyond that. The rubrics are purposefully made to be student friendly and to provide clear stepping stones from one level to the next. Students receive online resources, such as Raz-Kids (www.raz-kids.com), an online library of leveled readers. (Visit **go.SolutionTree.com/PLCbooks** to access live links to the websites mentioned in this book.) Students have the opportunity to choose the books they want, listen to them, read them, test their own comprehension, and get immediate feedback. Teachers also provide online video and reading resources that give students the scaffolding to meet the next target.

To provide students with a real-life language experience, teachers give students the opportunity for interaction with a variety of Spanish speakers. They work extensively to create a Spanish-speaking-parent volunteer program. In this program, Spanish speakers join the classrooms. As most students work in groups of two on different conversational tasks or projects, the native speakers simply sit and converse with the students. Teachers also encourage students to ask the volunteers a lot of questions about their lives and their country of origin. Student Voice: SAS Elementary Spanish shares one student's experience.

# SAS Early Learning Center

The members of the early learning center team at SAS have been engaged in a deeply reflective process that centers on raising the agency, participation, and authentic involvement of students. A rigorous investigation into innovative practices across different cultural contexts led the teachers to consider the Reggio Emilia educational

## Student Voice: SAS Elementary Spanish

My name is Johnny. I moved to Singapore from Vietnam. My parents think that speaking more than one language is very important. They can also speak several languages. When I came to the Singapore American School in grade 4, my family and I had the choice of a daily language program in Mandarin or Spanish. I chose Spanish, and entered the grade 4 novice class. In this daily, forty-five-minute class, I began learning the basics. "Hello! What is your name?" "Where are you from?" and "What languages do you speak?" were some of the beginning questions I learned to answer. The classroom space was divided into centers that provided games, obstacle courses, and practice around specific sets of questions. By the winter holiday, my teachers let me try out the intermediate class.

The teacher explained how to move up proficiency levels in the intermediate class by giving me a simple list as a rubric.

I liked the intermediate class, so the teachers let me stay. I began learning about Pablo Picasso, Real Madrid, and Barcelona in Spanish class. Every day my classmates and I worked in pairs to discuss the topics through games or special sets of toys. Sometimes we even got to use exercise equipment; we could stay on the exercise equipment for as long as we could keep talking in Spanish!

The next year, I started grade 5 in the intermediate class, but by the end of the first week, I was bumped up to the intermediate high class. In this high-level course, I learned that I needed to continue to speak in organized sentences, but that I also needed to be able to describe in detail and narrate in the past and future. I learned about Puerto Rico. One of my favorite things to study was the life of Roberto Clemente, because I like baseball. I practiced talking about his life and then compared or contrasted aspects of my life. My teacher wrote notes to help me with my verbs so that I knew how to speak correctly. Part of getting to I5 (intermediate high) is to use the right verbs in the right places, and it can get a bit tricky, especially in the past and future.

When I arrived in the middle school, I still had the same goal of I5. In grade 6, I learned about Mexico. We learned about Aztec legends, quinceañeras, mole (the food), and the biographies of famous Mexicans. I had to learn to narrate in the past and in the future and to describe with detail. By the end of grade 6, I received AAPPL scores of I5 and A (intermediate high and advanced low) in speaking, listening, reading, and writing. I am pretty excited, because my dad told me that if I got to intermediate high, he would take me with him on his next business trip to Barcelona. When I go to Barcelona, I want to go to the Sagrada Família, because I learned about it in grade 4. I also want to eat paella negra and tapas because my grade 4 Spanish teacher said that tapas were his favorite food in Spain, and learning about paella in class was really interesting to me.

project. Founded after World War II by psychologist Loris Malaguzzi, the Reggio Emilia approach situates itself around the "image of the child" who is understood to be competent, social, and resourceful, and endowed with rights from birth. Its premise is to value and make visible children's agency in all aspects of their learning and development.

Another of the key theories of Reggio Emilia is the concept of the hundred languages of children, a metaphor for the multiple ways that children think, express themselves, and understand and encounter others as they create connections among the various dimensions of the learning experience, rather than separate and compartmentalize them. It is an active process of participation that values the contributions of all stakeholders in the educational process: students, teachers, parents, and the school community.

Through sustained investigation, the SAS early learning team found resonance with the Reggio Emilia experience and philosophy. With the assistance of pedagogical consultant Fiona Zinn, the team embarked on a journey of intensive inquiry focused around three central questions: (1) What are the values underpinning the experience in Reggio Emilia? (2) How do these values resonate with our own cultural context at SAS? and (3) How might these experiences shape our teaching and learning practices?

During a two-year period, the team worked to deeply analyze its practice within its cultural context and the driving philosophy and pedagogical practices of Reggio Emilia. These sustained inquiries and the resulting program enhancement were far-reaching and transformative. The program's success required many important elements be in place, the most significant of which was the existence of a rigorous culture of professional reflection facilitated by the long-standing PLC climate within the school. As an end result, the SAS early childhood team has successfully created an environment where three- and four-year-olds are almost entirely personalizing their learning outcomes.

## Collaboration

Learning is a social process; it happens when individuals interact, communicate, listen, reflect, and generate new ideas in response to one another. If we believe that all children are competent learners, then we must also recognize the role of the competent teachers who look closely into their practice to understand the intricacies of the teaching and learning practices more deeply. The educators in Reggio Emilia recognize that just as students engage as protagonists in their own learning, so too must teachers. This requires a shift in the role of the teacher from an emphasis on teaching to an emphasis on learning—teachers learning about themselves as teachers as well as teachers learning about children.

As the teachers in the early learning center team engaged in reflective dialogue, the visibility they gave to learning and to their students' sense of agency began to emerge. The value of documenting learning from the perspective of "How are the children co-constructing knowledge?" rather than "What do they know?" gave rise to a new dialogue about learning that repositioned the four critical PLC questions at the center of the collaborative work.

## Critical Question 1: What Do I Want to Know, Understand, and Be Able to Do?

From a traditional education mindset, this first question might seem straightforward, easily answered, and useful as a springboard for future action; however, from a Reggio Emilia perspective, new layers of subjectivity start to emerge. Using this question at SAS, the early childhood educators were able to dig deeply into observing areas of interest, significant provocations, and stimuli for inquiry that might trigger a connection between prior knowledge and new possibilities for stimulating learning.

Based on the notion of a capable learner, teachers observe questions, interests, choices, interactions, theories, and representations of learning that serve as vital launching points into bigger conceptual investigations. Together, students and educators work to deduce hypotheses and formulate potential proposals for what *could* happen rather than to seek definitive explanations or simplify the process to the transmission of information.

SAS has clearly identified important learning targets based on 21st century learning skills: communication, collaboration, creativity, critical thinking, character, content knowledge, and cultural competence. In the early learning center, teachers see and strengthen these goals within important overarching conceptual themes: identity, community, environment, and symbolic communication (incorporating, among other things, inquiry into the coded systems of language and mathematics). Within the inquiry process, teachers look for potential links between students' interests and experience and the overarching conceptual themes.

For example, one teacher was in an outdoor learning area with a small group of students. The students were good friends and were experimenting with various pouring vessels around a tub filled with water. The teacher posed a challenge, asking the students how they might use the new materials she provided to explore the vessels in new ways. Immediately, a simple learning moment became a powerful learning moment.

Following is the students' conversation as they discuss with their teacher their theories on how to force water down a tube in the right direction. They watch while the water forces its way out when one end is lifted high and one end is dropped down low.

**Moriah:** Can I have a try? That is too much. Actually, it cannot go on her head.

**Amy:** I can feel the water!

**Amelia:** Can I have a try?

**Zali:** How about we can use this one? (*Zali changes the funnel to see if it will stick into the hose better.*)

**Moriah:** Can I have a try?

**Zali:** One by one, okay? (*Students take turns!*)

**Amelia:** Hold it up, up! Hey! Hold it up!

**Zali:** Okay.

**Amelia:** Like this (*stands up to show her*).

**Amelia:** No, it goes down itself. See that hole? It goes down.

The conversation continues.

**Teacher:** If the water goes down, where does it come out? Up high or down low?

**Amelia:** Down low. Sit down, Amy.

**Amy:** Your turn, Moriah. Sit down low.

**Amelia:** We're putting the water in. You pour it in and you move this (*indicates the hose*).

**Moriah:** Here comes some!

**Zali:** Yes! See! I pour the water in here and it comes out here!

This experiment took the students further into a knowledge of directionality, force, and movement, concepts connected to the overarching conceptual themes of community and environment.

## Critical Question 2: How Will I Demonstrate That I Have Learned It?

Borrowing from the emphasis on documenting learning in Reggio Emilia, we expand the potential of this PLC question. Shifting the focus from seeing this as an individual or personalized question to seeing it as a shared and co-constructed learning approach, educators at SAS now use this as a primary source of pedagogical strategy. Asking, "How do the students demonstrate their evolving understanding?" and "How are educators using the process of documentation to give value to the learning processes that arise?" extends the application of this PLC question in meaningful ways. Using the collected documentation, educators in the early learning center collaborate on, analyze, interpret, reflect on, and present possible points for revision.

Figure 7.2 (page 122) provides examples of collected documentation of student voice and the collaborative team's subsequent interpretations.

## Critical Question 3: What Will I Do When I Am Not Learning?

At Reggio Emilia, educators view practice and students through a lens of competency and capability. In this framework, the student is a capable learner, and it is the role of the educators to hear the student, see the student, and advocate for the student. Question 3, even when asked from a student's perspective, doesn't align with the educational project of Reggio Emilia. In fact, it would be an offense to suggest that a student can stop learning. So educators focus on questions such as, What can we do to actively tease out the "knots" (complications and challenges) in learning? How might students draw on the people around them to support this process? and How are the processes of teasing out tensions and projecting new intentions shaped by the relational experiences around the student?

## Critical Question 4: What Will I Do When I Have Already Learned It?

Reconsidering this question through a Reggio Emilia lens, the educators in the early learning center began to focus on the following: What can educators do to relaunch learning and extend the conceptual avenues of investigation? In what ways does the learning of the individual extend, shape, and adapt itself in response to the ideas, interactions, and shared learning of the group?

Born from the need for democratic exchange and dialogue, this process interrogates the reciprocity of the individual and the group, recognizing the agency of all participants during the process. Taking ownership of your own learning is one thing, but to take shared ownership and responsibility for shaping new directions in group thinking is another, albeit deeply interconnected, process. At SAS, the schoolwide emphasis on extraordinary care gives weight, shape, and context to the pedagogy of relationships in learning. Underpinning the entirety of the experience at SAS, this emphasis on understanding agentic relationships connects with Reggio Emilia as it recognizes, "Relationships (are) the fundamental organising strategy of our educational system" (Malaguzzi, 1993, p. 10, as cited in Fleer et al., 2006, p. 47).

| Documented Moment in Learning | Question Prompts for Interpretation |
|---|---|
| "Why is the bird's shell strong when the baby is inside the egg, but not strong when it is broken?"<br><br>"How do snails talk?" | What concepts can we see coming into this experience? Why is this significant, interesting, and challenging for these students? How has the learning process become visible through the documented piece? What is it about students' insatiable curiosity in the natural world that continually serves as a provocation for learning? How might we take this moment of inquiry further? |
| "The moon followed me to school today." | How do students' experiences outside the context of the early learning center shape their interest and dialogue in the classroom? How might different students interpret and interact with this experience? What narrative potentials can this bring to learning as we explore links between nonliving entities and behaviors? How might this small moment in learning allow teachers to tap into the imaginative and creative capacities of students? |
| "Can I have a turn?"<br><br>"I rolled the ball down and she [caught] it, we did a teamwork!" | How does the experience of learning in a group shape the way students express themselves? How do students encounter the shared experience and develop strategies for relating in this space? How does an experience such as this engender group behaviors? |
| "Remember how we learned that salt can stick them together? We can use that to make our own iceberg!" | How do students connect to prior knowledge? How does this prior knowledge shape experiences? What new "languages of expression, thinking, and communication" might we launch using this provocation? |
| "I need the box and we can make a house for the animals then all the animals will stay inside then they can have so much fun. They don't have any house. All the animals' house has break so we need another house, and this is the idea we can make this house." | What is the relationship between students' symbolic play and learning foundational literacy and numeracy skills? (For example, how does understanding that a box can represent a house later translate to an understanding that the letter *a* can represent the sound /a/?) |

**Figure 7.2:** Sample student voice documents and staff interpretations of student work.

Fiona Zinn gives insight into how the educational project of Reggio Emilia impacts the early learning team at SAS (F. Zinn, personal communication, 2015):

> Seeing Reggio Emilia as a provocation for renovating pedagogy and philosophy extends and challenges the PLC process in many important ways. Investigating, discussing, and experimenting with these ideas initiated a deeply reflective and collaborative process at SAS ELC. Considering the four PLC questions more intensely led the team to move beyond simple "I statements" and replace these with a "we" mindset. Instead of a linear recipe for addressing learning discrepancies, the PLC approach now presents a provocation for an intricate search for complex answers and sustained shared understanding. This process has deepened the daily pedagogical rigor at SAS ELC and raised the agency, visibility, and participation of children, educators, and the community.

These examples are but a few that we selected to demonstrate how various schools around the world are giving their youngest learners agency over their own learning. None of these examples are perfect, but they are authentic. Returning agency to students can be scary and uncomfortable at times, but these schools have found it to be foundational for powerful engagement and learning.

## Questions to Consider

Consider the following four questions as you begin your transformation to a highly effective and learning-progressive school.

1. **The learning:** What are the important learnings for me in this chapter? For my school? What am I inspired to know and be able to do?

2. **The evidence:** What are we already doing that aligns with this paradigm? What would change in my school and professional experience if we further embrace and implement it?

3. **The learning pit:** What obstacles would we face if we were to try or to further this approach? What strategies could we use to experience breakthroughs?

4. **The lever:** What would we need to accelerate the change process?

# 8

# From Theory
# to Practice in
# Middle Schools

In this chapter, we illustrate the personalized learning approach by sharing the stories of middle schools that are committed to offering programs that are highly effective and learning progressive. We hope these examples from middle schools will help you take steps to try something new in your school.

The core focus of these middle schools is the desire to give students agency over their own learning process. You will see examples of how middle schools are empowering students to ask and answer the four critical questions of a PLC for themselves. While some of the schools do not explicitly use the four critical questions of a PLC, all of them have an inquiry process that fits nicely within the PLC framework.

First, we share the story of the i-LEARN communities at Academia Cotopaxi in Quito, Ecuador. Then, we feature the stories of the Futures Academy at the International School of Beijing and Hobsonville Point School in Auckland, New Zealand.

## i-LEARN Communities at Academia Cotopaxi

Dan Kerr, the intermediate school principal at Academia Cotopaxi in Quito, Ecuador, has been wrestling with the idea of giving students agency in their learning through the PLC process for some time. Through much research into other schools implementing personalized learning and collaboration, he and his team have established i-LEARN communities, a structure that deliberately empowers students to ask and answer the critical questions of a PLC. The i-LEARN community initiative started as a pilot project in two classes. Dan and his team chose a grade 7 class and a grade 5 class to see how they could best implement this approach to student ownership across all grades the following year. i-LEARN is a personalized pathway experience that deliberately focuses on transdisciplinary learning outcomes for students. Each i-LEARN class meets once a week. Student Voices: i-LEARN Communities (page 127) relays the stories of students from the pilot program.

## Collaboration

The i-LEARN structure is purposely set up to ensure collaboration between students and teachers, teachers and teachers, and students and students. A student facilitator and a student timekeeper lead that day's session when students first get into their i-LEARN groups. These roles are rotating, much like in a PLC collaborative team. (Teachers model and teach many of Robert Garmston's strategies for collaborative group success, as well as the critical friends protocol, which gives students a sense of how these sessions should effectively run [Garmston & Wellman, 1999].) Teachers also frame the day's session around a particular driving question. The students take turns going through the facilitator-managed process, answering the session's driving question, giving feedback, responding to feedback, analyzing assessment data, making suggestions for areas of growth, and proposing strategies that will move the students forward. The session always ends with each student taking notes (oral or written) on the biggest takeaway from the session, and the new learnings or understandings that students learned from their group that day.

The teacher collaborates with each i-LEARN group throughout the forty-five minute or hourlong session as well. Teachers are very much in the role of active listener, there to ensure that the groups are not getting stuck or bogged down on any particular issue, and encouraging students to adhere to the protocols and processes of the structure. They have a clipboard, their smartphone, or a video camera in hand, and they are eager to take anecdotal notes on student concerns, student feedback, areas for growth, and strategies to move forward. They are doing a lot of listening and thinking, trying to find ways to help each individual student's learning. The teacher shares notes with each student during his or her individual conferencing session later that day or the next day. The teacher then leads a final reflection exercise at the end of the session that brings all the groups together to share their learning, to give final feedback, and to talk about next steps for the following week's session. Another big part of this final reflection exercise is to celebrate the failures of the groups to showcase how and why a particular student went wrong, to use these failures as pathways to success for others. Teachers try hard to make all the students' thinking visible and very much part of the learning process. This builds trust in the class, as well as with the students, and they

## Student Voices: i-LEARN Communities

My name is Stephen. I have been living in Quito, Ecuador, and attending Academia Cotopaxi for three years. My father works for a U.S. oil company, and this is our fourth international post as a family, and my third international school. I see myself as a typical middle school student. I enjoy music, sports, being with my friends, and traveling to new places. I am a good student, and I feel I do traditional school well. I know how to "play the game" in order to get good grades—I know how to study just the right amount to keep my teachers and parents happy. Lately, however, I have become more and more uninspired with school because of the lack of opportunities that I have to drive my own learning and to pursue my own passions. I am really passionate about service learning, and I am a driving force and leader in our Global Issues Network (GIN) conference planning committee, a regional conference to be held at our school. Lately, I have started to question the relevance of what I am being asked to learn, as I see it as not connecting to my day-to-day life as a middle school student. The i-LEARN structure has reignited my passion for learning, and because of this new structure, I have become re-engaged in school. For the first time in a long time I am truly enjoying my classes and my learning!

• • • • • • • •

My name is Sarah. I have been living in Quito, Ecuador, and attending Academia Cotopaxi for two years. My father works for a Canadian mining company, and this is our first international experience as a family, and my first time ever out of Canada. I feel like I am a very able student, and I absolutely love to learn. I see myself as self-directed, curious, and I am eager to devour as much new information about everything and anything as long as it interests me, which can be a problem. You see, I have become increasingly frustrated with school because I find it too easy, which is boring, and most of what I learn doesn't interest me at all. There haven't been many opportunities in the last couple of years to deepen and extend my learning. I feel like I have no choice or say in my education and that makes me sad. I really, really enjoy art and drama, and I love anything that allows me to be creative. My mom calls me a free spirit, which I take as a compliment. This year I am on our student leadership team, and I love to find ways to give back to our community, and to think about solutions to local issues (there are lots of these in Ecuador). The i-LEARN structure, however, has been freeing for me, and it has provided me with so many opportunities to "go deep" and to connect my love of learning with my personal passions. I am starting to love school again!

know that they are a team in the learning process. The teacher, of course, is always thinking, "How can I move each one of my students forward in his or her learning?"

Teachers then debrief with other teachers (in department team meetings or grade-level team meetings) to discuss their student notes with each other. They see if there are any emerging themes, or common struggles, or areas that stand out with the assessment data that they can dig deeply into and find solutions to. Much like PLC collaborative teams, when teachers collaborate, they focus on how to increase student learning, and how to use data (either anecdotal or concrete) to extend, intervene, or more effectively differentiate with their students. Teachers offer feedback to each other, suggest strategies to each other, provide resources to each other, and even offer to come and observe or videotape a lesson that one of their colleagues is teaching. It's a nice extension of the regular PLC model, and very much brings the students authentically into the discussion.

The collaborative opportunities within the i-LEARN structure are what make it so successful. These are never done in isolation, but rather in groups and teams, which allows for (and maximizes) opportunities for feedback, reflection, shared understanding, and ultimately student learning.

## Critical Question 1: What Do I Want to Know, Understand, and Be Able to Do?

Stephen walked into his i-LEARN community group session in mathematics class and took out his preassessment on the introduction of algebraic equations. He got into his group of four students, and they spent the next thirty minutes looking at each other's assessments. They discussed the teacher's feedback, shared the mistakes that they made, helped each other understand the concepts from different perspectives, and focused on the thinking behind how it was possible to arrive at the right answer in different ways. Stephen left the session with a much clearer understanding of where he needed to go in his learning, and he was better set up to drive his learning over the following weeks.

This was the first time that Stephen had ever shared an assessment with anyone else other than his teacher and parents, and at first he was nervous. Like most middle school students, he was unsure how his peers would react to seeing his many mistakes; he thought they would judge him negatively. The teacher worked hard over the preceding months to help students understand the idea of growth mindsets (Dweck, 2006) and that the real learning comes from making mistakes and sharing them with the group. He had been using a lot of education author and professor of mathematics education at the Stanford Graduate School of Education Jo Boaler's thinking (Boaler, Chen, Williams, & Cordero, 2016) around mathematics instruction, and he'd been preparing the students for this group activity of data sharing. Since this was a preassessment, he framed the activity around using these initial data to help lead the individual student learning process as students moved forward in the unit.

After the session, Stephen commented that it was actually really cool and really helpful to see that his peers had made similar mistakes, and that he now trusts his classmates a lot more. He noticed that he better understands the concepts because his peers spoke to him in student-friendly language that the teacher sometimes forgot to use when he shared his assessment with them. They had so much patience, and it was fun for him to help teach one of his group members something that only he knew. He left feeling empowered and successful, and the last thing he said as he walked out the door was, "That math class was actually fun!" The driving question that this i-LEARN session addresses at the beginning of each unit or lesson is, What do I want to know, understand, and be able to do?

## Critical Question 2: How Will I Demonstrate That I Have Learned It?

Stephen walked into his i-LEARN community group session in social studies class and immediately opened up his computer and logged on to Skype (https://web.skype .com). He was three weeks into a unit on conflict, and he was about to reach out to his critical friends group, which his teacher had organized through a personalized learning network. His critical friends group consisted of himself, a seventh-grade boy at the American School of London named Martin, and a seventh-grade girl at the American International School of Lagos named Jenny. This was the third time that they'd met virtually, and today they would share their reflections of their learning so far around the ideas of conflict.

They all shared their portfolio blog links with each other; and later, they took turns showcasing their learning, their formative assessment feedback, their hard wonderings (the things they really wanted to know more about), and the unit's connection to their personal lives. It was a rich learning session for Stephen as he heard all about how Jenny and her family (and the school) were dealing with the current rebel conflict in Nigeria, and the experiences of Martin's grandfather during the Vietnam War when he was a tunnel rat for just over a year. Stephen shared his own experience in Quito, where protesters had been gathering to protest the current government and how students had been sent home early due to the potential riots.

It was amazing for Stephen to share his reflections with his peers from all over the world, and he commented that he never thought that his best teachers would be his own peers! They spent a little time talking about where to go next in their learning, and they shared their biggest takeaways so far from the unit. They set up a date for the following week to talk about how they planned to showcase and demonstrate their learning, which goes along with this i-LEARN driving question that Stephen had been thinking about: How will I demonstrate that I have learned it? which meant he asked himself, "What will I produce to demonstrate mastery of my intended learning target (formatively along the way, and as a summative piece)?"

## Critical Question 3: What Will I Do When I Am Not Learning?

Sarah sat down in her i-LEARN community to specifically think about her primary years program (PYP) exhibition of learning presentation that was coming up in a couple of weeks. Her group consisted of three other students, who, like Sarah, were all passionate about the issue of homelessness in Ecuador and all over the world. They had been researching this topic for over a month and were now at a point where they weren't sure how to take the next step in their learning. They had been going through the design thinking process as a group (Kelley & Littman, 2007), and they had come up with some solution-focused ideas that would hopefully effect positive change in the local community, but then they got a little stuck about how to move forward. They weren't clear on how to bring their action plan to life, and they couldn't agree on how to demonstrate their learning on the actual night of the community presentation. They related their struggles to the i-LEARN driving question, What will I do when I am not learning? That meant asking questions like the following.

- "What resources do I have to use to get unstuck in my learning?"

- "What strategies can I call on?"

- "What questions can I ask of myself, my peers, or my teacher?"

As a group, they started brainstorming ideas about what they should do, and their teacher sat in and listened to their ideas and thinking. Sarah suggested that they take their questions to their mentor teacher (all PYP exhibition of learning groups have a mentor teacher who meets with them on occasion to help with the process) and that they sit in on some other group meetings to give them ideas to move forward. The rest agreed, and they spent the next twenty minutes or so sitting in on other groups' conversations. Members took notes, listened intently, and thought of how the other project approaches might be useful to them. After a while, they headed back to their table and started throwing ideas around, and it came out that one group's idea for a website and fundraising campaign inspired Sarah and her groupmates. They started discussing the event of an earthquake on Ecuador's coast, and Sarah suggested that they use this terrible event to highlight the increased homelessness that Ecuador was now experiencing. They decided to begin a relief campaign that included collecting clothing, money, and nonperishable food, which would go to assist not only the people on the coast but the people of Quito proper as well. They successfully took the next step in their learning by finding different ways to engage in their project, and by working together collaboratively to get unstuck. Sarah commented that it is funny how a single good idea could transfer to many different situations—good learning indeed!

## Critical Question 4: What Will I Do When I Have Already Learned It?

Sarah and four other classmates got into their i-LEARN community group to end the week on Friday afternoon. They had all been individually writing reflections in their blogs, which was part of their electronic portfolio, throughout the week, and now it was time to share. That day, they read each other's reflections and consolidated the week's learning into one final reflection that members would craft together for their final weekly blog post. They were framing the conversation around the i-LEARN driving question, What will I do when I have already learned it? That meant asking questions like the following.

- "What is the next thing I need to learn?"

- "How can I extend my learning and pursue my interests?"

- "How can I connect my learning to real life? How can I dig deeper?"

They took turns reading their reflections about mathematics, PYP, and literacy, as well as their learning in their specialist classes. Sarah said that she loved these end-of-week reflection sessions because she always came away with some new learning and some new ideas that she hadn't connected with on her own. She said that sometimes her greatest learning throughout the week was listening to the different perspectives and thoughts of her friends. Sarah loved to be the scribe when they came up with the final joint reflection post. It made her proud to be in this leadership role. She always made sure that they ended the post with questions about where they could next take their learning individually and as a group, and a plan around how to do that. Sarah thought that the most fun part was connecting their week's learning to their own lives, and she loved to tell stories about how she saw her learning as relevant. With about five minutes to go, their group members shared their biggest learning from the week from any class, and then they all went off to the weekend knowing that the week had been full of incredible learning!

Sarah said that the i-LEARN sessions were the best part of her week because she now had an opportunity to drive her own learning and share her reflections on her learning, and she had other students who could help her dive deep and extend what she wanted to know. She commented, "I didn't know I could learn so much from my friends! My teachers are smart, but I think that my friends are smarter!"

# Futures Academy at the International School of Beijing

Former academy coordinator Kyle Wagner and his team at the International School of Beijing have undertaken a huge challenge as they set out to design the middle school of the future. They asked, "What would school look like if students and their learning were at the center of our school design?" Futures Academy started off as a grand experiment and is now a featured program with a waiting list of students ready to participate in a whole new approach to learning. Futures Academy is a comprehensive and self-contained program that allows middle school students to master essential middle school disciplinary, transdisciplinary, and personalized learning outcomes through a personalized learning pathway and personalized learning progression experience. Student Voice: Futures Academy features a student's story.

### Student Voice: Futures Academy

My name is Johnny. I am a grade 8 student in the Futures Academy at the International School of Beijing. I come to school early, before the sun has fully risen, to fuss with my Arduino—the microcontroller (miniature brain) I use to manipulate small robots. My friend Cliff arrives to school early as well to configure new levels for a video game he is designing. He watches some YouTube videos to find ideas and transfers the information into a Word document to dictate player commands.

Other students file in and take their seats among the comfortable furniture around the room. Some sit and discuss the latest teenage gossip on red beanbags while others rock from side to side on specially designed chairs intended to improve student engagement. While I'm not that into teenage gossip, I certainly love the flexible furniture.

After a brief reminder from the facilitators that mentoring is to start in a minute, I close my screen and roll my chair to a group circle where Futures Academy meets at the beginning of each day. Facilitators and students welcome us to the group, and we then share a topic of interest. I then close my eyes for the next activity, which helps frame student learning for that day. Three students the facilitator are *tappers*, students who tap the shoulders of students who embody the characteristics the facilitators list. I crack a grin when I am tapped on the shoulder for being one of the most innovative students in the class. The activity continues for another five minutes with the final category embodying the class's most effective presenters. Once the final students are tapped, we all open our eyes. I listen as the humanities facilitator asks these last four students to help lead a schoolwide poetry café in the cafeteria, giving students an opportunity to share their favorite poems as well as read their own.

Mentoring ends with one of my classmates reading the schoolwide, daily announcements and the facilitators giving a brief overview of the day. I then gather my materials for humanities while a few of my good friends gather their supplies for science, which is held on the opposite side of the movable whiteboards stretched across the room. Facilitators determine the groups based on our project work in each class. In science, we are in the midst of finishing designs and learning the physics principles behind our Rube Goldberg machines; while in humanities, we are in stage two of an integrated project with Chinese that asks students to experience life from another's perspective. After I take my seat, my humanities teacher asks me to observe symbols for five major world religions. Ultimately, we will be responsible for understanding how religion impacts a given person's daily life to create our "life-in-a-day" video, filmed from our global character's perspective.

I find that I know much more about Christianity than other Eastern religions, which is troublesome given that my global character is from Tibet. Fortunately, there are a few members in my small group who also practice Buddhism, and are therefore able to provide some guidance on how this religion might impact my life.

Meanwhile, on the other side of the whiteboards dividing the room, our science facilitator is giving a dynamic lesson in physics, teaching properties of motion so that groups will be more successful in the design of their own Rube Goldberg machines. And while this particular lesson is not integrated with what is happening in humanities, a flexible schedule allows me to get more individualized attention and instruction. In fact, after about forty minutes of exploring religion's effects on daily life, rather than moving to the next class, my facilitators switch places and deliver the same lesson to my small group. For example, while it's a bit of a stretch, my science facilitator can relate forces and motions to the invisible factors that influence daily life.

continued →

After the blended mathematics and humanities block, I take a short break, where I have the opportunity to mix with the students outside of Futures Academy. The "geek squad," as we call our group of friends, is eager to discuss new video games and the nanotechnology we read about in *Popular Science*.

After the break, I return to class where I find my classmates huddled in a circle around a blank whiteboard. My facilitator asks us to brainstorm activities to complete during our flexible block of time, a period for us to catch up on our project work or work toward our SMART goals set around our greatest needs. Although I love mathematics, I find working on mathematics is less relevant than building my skills in humanities, specifically related to vocabulary. While I have enjoyed my current piece of writing in humanities, it lacks the diversity of word choice to engross the reader. When prompted, I share "vocabulary development" as a possible activity. Ultimately, the board is filled with six sample activities that I need to complete during the flexible block.

Having identified a humanities-related goal, I seek my humanities facilitator's support in consulting the appropriate vocabulary-enrichment app. My teacher sits next to me and shows me a site that moves at the user's pace. Together, we set a realistic goal of how much to complete during the flexible time. After about twenty-five minutes of work on vocabulary enrichment, I take a self-imposed break to grab some water and fresh air outside. I return after a few minutes to find my mathematics facilitator took the free seat beside my empty chair.

Similar to humanities, I recently developed a SMART goal related to mathematics, which was tough given my current level of mastery. Fortunately, my facilitator has other resources at his disposal. At the beginning of the year, he introduced my whole class to a dynamic and intuitive online tool called Khan Academy (www.khanacademy.org). This free course allowed us to self-direct our learning, moving at a pace appropriate to our level of mathematics mastery. I knew that while my number sense was strong, I could always work on my spatial-visual skills, a topic crucial to understanding ninth-grade mathematics. After reviewing my progress on the other strands, I entered the course Manipulating Shapes. Together with my facilitator, we set a goal to complete ten of the introductory problems, which include a brief video tutorial embedded within the course content.

## Collaboration

Collaboration is at the heart of the Futures Academy program. Its focus on integration and preparing students for a rapidly changing global society means that collaboration is essential to the program's success. Collaboration is not just encouraged; it's mandated. The program has carved out collaborative teacher meeting times for every day of the six-day cycle. Four days of the week are for grade-level-specific team meetings, while two days are for whole-team meetings. Given their level of infrequency, whole-team meetings are carefully planned with clear agendas and outcomes driving the discussions, while smaller grade-level-team meetings are more flexible, weighing the project's needs.

Grade-level meetings should focus on integrating subject-specific material and authentic experiences around the project's needs, rather than the minutia of the curriculum. This unique approach has allowed integration to happen naturally, rather than being forced. Conversations usually involve previewing the week's integrated lessons, which understandably take up half of the student's time, as well as planning tasks and activities to help support the learning. Because of the program's unique size, with only seven facilitators and seventy students spread across two grade levels, the program can evolve dynamically and rapidly, able to change direction and focus if certain approaches are not working.

The anecdotal story about Johnny provides an insight into the dynamic relationship between teacher and student in this model. Given the daily infusion of self-directed learning, teachers in Futures Academy must take on a new role. Rather than being the great disseminators of course content, they act instead as facilitators of learning, able to guide students to self-imposed objectives and goals. Facilitators use dynamic tools to maintain this relationship. Comprehensive online programs help chart out paths for student learning in a far more effective way than the teacher, with the ability to target problems according to students' specific needs. Facilitators in this model act as coaches to ensure students are moving at an appropriate pace. When misunderstandings do occur, they are able to lead small-group and one-on-one minilessons to clear things up. With Futures Academy's all-hands-on-deck model, the teacher-to-pupil ratio is decreased, allowing for smaller grouping of students and in turn more individualized instruction. Lastly, in the context of the larger integrated unit, facilitators, according to their content expertise, infuse the skills where they naturally fit to help ensure students are meeting standards.

Student-to-student relationships are also crucial to Futures Academy's success. The unique community acts much like a family. This is because students are together for most of the day with only a brief break for enrichments and language courses in the middle of the day. This frequency of interaction allows them to develop relationships and a comfort level that are integral to success in their challenging projects.

Futures Academy has instituted strategic structures within the program to help foster these relationships between students. Most notable among these is daily mentoring. Every day begins with mentoring in order to establish the framework for the day, and to allow students to connect to one another. It has also instituted student-run committees to foster student-to-student interaction. These small committees range from facility oversight to the planning of social events. By handing over control of management to students, students feel a greater ownership of the space.

Finally, Futures Academy helps foster student-to-student relationships through constant reflection on collaborative projects and group work. The typical "soft" skills of relationships, generally reserved as an afterthought in traditional curricular planning, are at the core of project development. Facilitators teach these skills explicitly and reflect together with students on how to best interact with their peers.

## Critical Question 1: What Do I Want to Know, Understand, and Be Able to Do?

The framing of student questions usually begins in the context of a project. Let's return to our student, Johnny, to see how Futures Academy empowered him to own his learning.

When Johnny learned the driving question at the beginning of the unit—How do we use cinematography to show what it's like to experience life in another person's shoes?—along with his character from Tibet, he knew he had a lot of questions to answer in order to successfully meet the project's end goal. Given the focus on film, he immediately identified his prior skills. He had completed film projects as tutorials for some of the tech tools he created. He knew these experiences might come in handy for filming the final project. However, after watching some *National Geographic* videos depicting the daily lives of different cultures, he realized he needed to know how to use various camera angles, dialogue, lighting effects, and other techniques to really make his video impactful. He also knew that he had to conduct a lot of research in social studies in order to fully understand what life is like in the hills of Tibet. He had to have an understanding of how geography, politics, religion, and society influence daily life. Finally, he knew that he would need to develop his foundational skills in descriptive writing, as he would need these skills to effectively narrate his character's story.

Johnny knew he would have to acquire other knowledge and skills; however, he would seek the experience of the facilitators in helping to frame his inquiries given his limited understanding of the project's scope.

## Critical Question 2: How Will I Demonstrate That I Have Learned It?

Given the integrated nature of projects in Futures Academy, Johnny had to integrate the skills he learned to demonstrate mastery in the integrated task. He would demonstrate this mastery through the synthesis of several specific learning targets he identified through critical question 1. Through continual formative self-reflection and self-assessment, Johnny would identify where he was succeeding in his learning journey and where he needed extra support. He would know he had achieved mastery of the intended learning target when he presented his summative piece to an authentic audience and articulated each stage of the learning process.

In more self-directed learning existing outside the project, Johnny would demonstrate mastery with continual check-ins with facilitators, using data from the online curriculum and goals he established earlier as a guide.

## Critical Question 3: What Will I Do When I Am Not Learning?

Given the unique approach to learning in Futures Academy, Johnny had several opportunities to demonstrate mastery, including many scheduled check-ins in the process of moving toward mastering integrated content. Through feedback sessions with classmates and experts in the field of study (in this case videographers, reporters, and anthropologists), Johnny could analyze exactly what was causing his block in learning and work collaboratively to address the disparity. In addition, with weekly goal setting and individualized learning, Johnny could work with his facilitator to acknowledge gaps and set goals for improvement.

## Critical Question 4: What Will I Do When I Have Already Learned It?

Establishing baseline data on every student at the onset of Futures Academy allowed Johnny to move at a pace appropriate to his level of knowledge and skills. Cognitive tests like the Measures of Academic Progress (MAP) and more flexible diagnostics built into Khan Academy established Johnny's baseline data and mapped out a learning path according to his abilities. Where online programs didn't meet his needs, Johnny relied on his own ability to chart his learning through one-on-one sessions with his facilitators with the diagnostic data as a guide for the conversation. To extend his learning and pursue his own interests, Johnny had two blocks a week, each ninety minutes in length, for his passion projects. At the beginning of the year, he barely understood how to program; by the end, he was building websites from scratch and programming Arduinos to manipulate complex robots.

# Hobsonville Point School

Hobsonville Point is a paradigm-shifting school that sits on the outskirts of Auckland, New Zealand. It is a public K–8 school that serves a very socioeconomically and culturally diverse community and is accountable to the national curriculum (Ministry of Education, 2007). Under the leadership of Principal Daniel Birch, the school made a deliberate choice to give students agency over their own learning. The outcome was quite remarkable. Hobsonville expects students to demonstrate mastery of essential disciplinary outcomes, transdisciplinary outcomes, and personalized learning outcomes in an entirely personalized learning environment. Student Voice: Hobsonville Point features one student's experience.

## Collaboration

The school leaders and educators at Hobsonville believe that positive relationships are the key to a student's success. Their students develop long-lasting, deep relationships with the adults they are working with, who they usually stay with for three to four years. Collaboration is one of Hobsonville's learning values. It believes that students learn best when they have multiple ways of knowing, so having access to a range of experts is very important. It believes that collaboration between students and collaboration with teachers are essential for creating a healthy learning environment.

In order to support a collaborative culture, the leaders at Hobsonville Point have put a number of support structures and tools in place. Becoming good at collaboration is not left to chance, and training and support are essential. These systems and resources guide the aforementioned collaboration between students and collaboration with teachers.

## Critical Question 1: What Do I Want to Know, Understand, and Be Able to Do?

Hobsonville valued conversations with students as its main process for giving students agency. Teachers knew students "don't know what they don't know," so learning was co-constructed with them to build knowledge and understanding. It valued the whole child, which included noticing students' passions, and helping them develop

## Student Voice: Hobsonville Point

My name is Julie, and I am a seventh grader. I arrive at school at eight in the morning. I come on my bike so I can ride it around when we have a break from learning. I always try to get here by 8 a.m. so I can start my learning before the 9 a.m. start. The first thing I do is connect with my teachers. I have two teachers who work with me. Once I am done, I get my planning for the day sorted. We have an online-planning site where the teachers put the work for the day. Each day can be different, so we all look forward to seeing what might be happening that day.

The day usually has a range of different activities. We always have workshops. Teachers, students, parents, or outside experts can run these workshops. Sometimes teachers assign us to a specific workshop, sometimes we choose to be in a workshop, and sometimes we don't even attend one. Other parts of the day we get to choose, especially if we are working on a project or inquiry. We might also be attending workshops in another learning hub or even attending classes at the high school.

Every day, I have to see one of my teachers to discuss my day and have him or her check off on my planning. The teacher always looks to see if I have balance in my plan for the day. The teacher also asks me about my previous day to see if I have made progress on my learning and to see if I am challenging myself. If my day involves collaborating with other students, then I always make sure I check in with them before getting my planning checked off. I am able to plan by myself in the morning, although I am still collaborating with my teachers so they can check off on my planning, which has only just happened for me. Before this, I planned my day with the teachers. I have demonstrated to them now that I can manage this process on my own.

As the day begins, those of us who have shown self-directed learning skills often begin by doing what we are interested in then. Other students may require support in managing their day. I used to need support, but now I have developed the skills to manage it myself. We have breaks during the day, but if we want we can keep working through them. We are allowed to eat, or take lunch, and get a drink when we need to. I also have a trust license, which allows me to work in different parts of the school with no adult support. So if I need the science room or the music room, I can go there for my learning. Throughout the day, the teachers I work with check up on me, but we can also have a conference where we share our learning. That conference also gets emailed home so my mom and dad know what I have been working on.

At the end of the day we always do a reflection. I don't really like this part of the day. But I do know why I need to do it. It really helps me focus for the next day and make sense of what I might need to focus on or even work on at home. I also email my reflections home so that my parents can see them.

understanding about themselves as learners so that they articulate or communicate their passions, interests, and needs.

The New Zealand Curriculum (Ministry of Education, 2007) is a powerful document that guides schools, like Hobsonville, in developing their own localized curriculum:

> The curriculum gives schools the scope, flexibility, and authority they need to design and shape their curriculum so that teaching and learning is meaningful and beneficial to their particular communities of students. In turn, the design of each school's curriculum allows teachers the scope to make interpretations in response to the particular needs, interests, and talents of individuals and groups of students in their classes. (p. 37)

With knowledge from the curriculum and of student progressions along with a well-developed teacher tool box to differentiate practice around student needs, staff were able to personalize learning that was targeted to both support and stretch each learner. Hobsonville used a conceptual curriculum to immerse students in *worlds of new* and then watch them create *wonderings*—what they want to learn and be able to do. Students then used these wonderings as a basis for inquiry as teachers guided them with scaffolding. Hobsonville students progressed through the continuum with three levels of scaffolding.

1. **Supported:** Students who need more scaffolding of learning and participate in supported inquiry from the teacher

2. **Self-managed:** Students who need a co-constructed learning approach where both teacher and student create the inquiry, which includes milestones and scaffolds

3. **Self-directed:** Students who identify both their needs and strengths and design their plan, with staff providing challenge and, where necessary, support through new learning

With constant conferencing and sharing of data (both visually on walls and personally), students were always part of the process of knowing what they may need to know next. Hobsonville used visual progressions on the walls of the learning space as trackers and points of reference, to mark milestones, and for reflection and goal setting.

## Critical Question 2: How Will I Demonstrate That I Have Learned It?

At Hobsonville, students and teachers had constant conferencing opportunities. These influenced the learning design for each student, and teachers and students shared them with parents. Students also had an individual education meeting once a term or when the need arose. These were where students celebrated their academic and dispositional growth and could help co-construct their new learning pathway, share their inquiry and their passions, and reflect on literacy and numeracy goals in comparison to national standards.

At Hobsonville, students had autonomy over how they demonstrate success or mastery. For academic learning areas, teachers and students utilized both formative and summative data to make judgments as to where they were in terms of curriculum levels. Teachers used approved, required standardized assessments along with other assessments, conversations with students, and student work samples to gauge progress. The teacher drove most assessment; however, student ownership of assessment was a key element of the system. Staff included students in all aspects of conversations around assessment. This made assessment purposeful and meaningful for students, and they developed a strong sense of ownership.

Students had multiple ways to demonstrate their knowledge and understanding. They could choose to teach another student, run a workshop, make a presentation, create or make something, or pass an assessment. All these demonstrations were done in consultation with the teacher, and the teacher used them to determine next steps for learning so students either stretched their learning, consolidated learning (deepening their understanding), or received support.

For dispositional learning, students used a learner profile to self-assess and provide evidence of their growth. Student-led conferences gave students the opportunity to prove where they believed they were and why. Negotiation between the teacher and the student determined where the student's final position was on the learning progression. This took into account the teacher's understanding of the learners' development, curriculum needs, and an intimate knowledge of students' holistic growth.

## Critical Question 3: What Will I Do When I Am Not Learning?

Hobsonville embraced student-friendly language (such as the *learning pit*) to help students identify when they were stuck in their learning. The school deliberately equipped students to get out of the pit. Students knew that imagination, grit, and questioning were tools to support moving out of it and finding success. Students understood that these qualities (as identified in the learner profile) helped them with group and individual goal setting. The school didn't expect students to automatically demonstrate the skills and qualities; students were taught what the qualities were, how to develop them, and, most important, how to know when they were in use and when they were not.

Students at Hobsonville used the language of supported, self-managed, and self-directed scaffolding to help identify the multiple forms of support that were available to them, from both teachers and students. A student may have noticed on a visual progression that another student had mastered something, so he or she could be a support as well. Sometimes, the teacher's role was simply to help identify other students as experts.

Since students had access to and knowledge of all data, they owned their progress and knew where they were as a learner, both academically and dispositionally. All learning information was highly visible around the school for students, teachers, and parents to see so next steps were easily identifiable.

## Critical Question 4: What Will I Do When I Have Already Learned It?

At Hobsonville, students co-constructed rubrics so they could self-assess as well as identify next steps. These rubrics could be around dispositions, skills, or the academic curriculum. During this co-construction, students and teachers unpacked what each level of achievement might look like, identified scaffolds that could support the learning, developed or shared examples of what supports might look like, and illustrated skill sets matched to the levels. By creating this big-picture overview in the context of connected inquiry and curriculum, students had the chance to dig deep, developed meaningful learning, and moved to more sophisticated levels as appropriate or necessary for them.

As with the previous chapter, these examples were selected to demonstrate how various schools around the world are giving their middle school students agency over their own learning. Giving middle school students room to wonder, try, fail, and learn could seem outright foolish to some, but these schools have found that this is exactly the environment middle school students need to engage and learn at the highest levels.

## Questions to Consider

Consider the following four questions as you begin your transformation to a highly effective and learning-progressive school.

1. **The learning:** What are the important learnings for me in this chapter? For my school? What am I inspired to know and be able to do?

2. **The evidence:** What are we already doing that aligns with this paradigm? What would change in my school and professional experience if we further embrace and implement it?

3. **The learning pit:** What obstacles would we face if we were to try or to further this approach? What strategies could we use to experience breakthroughs?

4. **The lever:** What would we need to accelerate the change process?

# 9

# From Theory
# to Practice in
# High Schools

In this chapter, we feature the stories of three high schools that have embraced a personalized learning approach and are committed to offering programs to students that are highly effective and learning progressive. We hope these examples from real high schools will inspire you to try something new in your school.

Each of these high schools has a desire to give students agency over their own learning process. You will see examples of how high schools are empowering students to ask and answer the four critical questions of a PLC for themselves. While some of the schools do not explicitly use the four critical questions of a PLC, all of them have an inquiry process that fits nicely within the PLC framework.

First, we share the story of NuVu Studio. Then, we move on to the Quest program. Finally, we explore Project X at the International Community School of Addis Ababa and the senior catalyst program at Singapore American School.

## NuVu Studio

As soon as you walk into the NuVu building, you realize it is no ordinary school. Besides being located adjacent to the Massachusetts Institute of Technology campus in Cambridge, Massachusetts, NuVu's design studio–like learning environment communicates that this is a school that fully engages students in authentic, hands-on learning from the start. At NuVu, students put theory into practice. Led by Saba Ghole, its cofounder and chief creative officer, NuVu is leading the charge in changing education from something that *happens to* students to a process that puts student engagement and ownership of learning at the center of its learning paradigm to equip students to enter an ever-increasing project-based world. NuVu clearly uses personalized learning pathways and personalized learning progressions to allow students to focus on transdisciplinary learning outcomes. This is NuVu's story.

See Student Voice: NuVu Studio for one student's experience.

### Student Voice: NuVu Studio

My name is Sara. I am fourteen years old. I decided to leave the traditional school system because I was uninspired and increasingly bored in class. During the school day, I would often doodle and sketch as a way to transport myself to an imaginary world that was without limits, full of color and depth. I am told that I have an inquisitive nature, but this inquisitiveness was slowly and gently being suppressed. I felt as if my questions were becoming a burden to the class, rather than the start of meaningful discussions.

I came to NuVu looking for a different experience, one that challenged me and allowed my creativity to flow. After spending a year here, I find myself growing above even my expectations, moving beyond the visual arts, in which I am naturally strong, and improving my engineering and technology skills.

Today is day seven of the Hacking Wheelchairs for Urbanity (https://goo.gl/owoJEL; NuVu, 2018) studio at NuVu. Twelve of my classmates and I are examining the challenges wheelchair users face in urban environments and developing low-cost solutions to improve their daily experiences and enable better integration with the rest of society. The Hacking Wheelchairs for Urbanity studio is one of sixteen studios NuVu is offering in its cities-themed trimester.

I begin the day with a quick recap with my teammate Karam. We discuss some challenges of the latest prototype for our wheelchair hand drive, a system that allows the wheelchair user to move faster with an unorthodox rowing motion that also exercises different muscles. We discuss a new iteration of our free-wheel mechanism. The NuVu coaches who are leading the studio, Chris and Rana, approach our team for the first of many daily *deskcrits*, in which they ask questions and offer feedback on our progress. As a group, we discuss ideas for the free-wheel mechanism. We decide to spend the day producing a 3-D model and then 3-D printing the parts for testing.

By the afternoon, the parts are printed, and we dive straight into assembly. We spend most of the afternoon in the workshop. During an early test, I realize we've made a critical mistake: the free wheel doesn't come out of the adapter piece. After a good deal of prying, it eventually pops out. We mount all the components to the wheelchair: the rod adapter, the rod, a ninety-degree turn for the arm, and the spider adapter.

We are ready to perform an advanced test. I sit in the wheelchair with the hand drive mounted to the wheel, and gently push the handle. I don't apply much force, but it cracks. I push harder and it breaks completely. The pieces fly everywhere!

We check in once again with our coaches toward the end of the day. Their feedback affirms the team's conclusion: our design was too brittle. For the next iteration, we decide to add thicker mounting legs and introduce a higher infill for the 3-D-printed parts to make the parts stronger.

We end the day documenting our day's work. Our blog post includes a detailed summary of our design decisions, iterations, and failures. It comprises a synthesis of what we have learned and our projections for tomorrow, another day of modifying and refining our design for the hand drive.

## Collaboration

Collaboration was central to the NuVu system. A solitary coach rarely led a studio; most involved two or more of these experts. These coaches were selected because of their diverse backgrounds and unique, specialized skill sets. NuVu built the decision to assign a team of coaches to a particular studio on those skills and how well the coaches' backgrounds complemented one another.

One of the two-week studios, Health and Wearable Tech, had two coaches. Rosa was an architect and fashion designer, and Robin was a roboticist. This combination fulfilled the studio's complex needs: students would be designing wearable products for users who are dealing with various challenges, and it would incorporate interactive and robotic elements.

At NuVu, students rarely, if ever, worked alone. The goal was to bring students together to explore ideas and solve problems. NuVu students came from different schools, different towns and cities, and different socioeconomic backgrounds. Typically, they worked in teams of two to three students of varying ages. The Health and Wearable Tech studio, for instance, had twelve students and two coaches. There were four to six student teams, each approaching the studio's goal in a unique way, with the group's diversity aiding it.

The start of every two-week studio began with group discussion and brainstorming around the given topic. Additional experts were often brought into the studio to share their real-world experiences with the students and help identify problem areas. Led by the coaches, these discussions usually generated broader project ideas and themes that the group shared collectively. After these discussions and team assignments, students developed ideas, built prototypes, synthesized additional feedback from their coaches and outside experts, and continuously iterated until they had a satisfactory solution.

## Critical Question 1: What Do I Want to Know, Understand, and Be Able to Do?

At NuVu, students learned how to use their creativity to take their own ideas and manifest them in real products. The process was challenging and involved the critical application of knowledge from many disciplines to identify and solve a real-world problem. This included high levels of mathematics, physics, writing, and coding, to name a few. Within each studio, students learned how to use a range of software and tools to help support their process and prototype their idea, including 3-D-modeling software, 3-D printers, and laser cutters.

Students didn't learn in discrete subject categories. Instead, they learned how to think about big, real, and comprehensive problems, and how to frame their thinking to find effective solutions. NuVu encouraged students to think critically. Student prototypes improved from the fresh information and feedback they were receiving every day. Students learned how to work in teams in which there were always differing ideas and points of view. Every two-week studio culminated in a final presentation and review when each team presented its project to a larger audience. The end-of-studio presentation and review helped students develop their oral communication skills and present their work with increasing confidence and clarity.

## Critical Question 2: How Will I Demonstrate That I Have Learned It?

NuVu's philosophy was about process and product. A rigorous design process ensured students went through multiple explorations at each stage. Students documented their design decisions at each stage to demonstrate their understanding of the project and their own response to the problem. This meant that each day, students collected assets (photos, screenshots, diagrams, videos, and so on) of the prototypes they were developing, reflected on their design decisions, and discussed how these design decisions addressed their main concept.

NuVu students also experienced an intense, feedback-rich environment that provided them with information and support for continuous self-evaluation, reflection, and improvement. Throughout the two-week studio, students were taking part in deskcrits and reviews with coaches and experts. During the deskcrits, students discussed their progress with coaches who assessed the students' thinking around the project and how they had realized their ideas through iterative prototyping.

At the end of the studio, the final presentation and review was a key moment. Each team presented its final product and shared a synthesis of the process that enabled the product's creation. This was how coaches and students assessed mastery of the design process and how students used feedback to improve their decisions.

## Critical Question 3: What Will I Do When I Am Not Learning?

The entire NuVu process focused on building competency around a process for dealing with open-ended problems. Many new students entered NuVu from very traditional learning environments where they were accustomed to giving the "right answer." In an open-ended, problem-based environment, there are instead many possible answers. Students learned how to navigate this process because they participated in several studios every trimester, and they learned how to move ahead when they were stuck. In such a situation, students might seek out a coach to get feedback on their progress, sketch alternative ideas for their prototype with their teammate, ask a peer for support on modeling part of their prototype, or learn how to use a sensor by finding resources online. Going through this process again and again helped students become more self-reliant to home in on their creative problem-solving skills.

## Critical Question 4: What Will I Do When I Have Already Learned It?

Unlike at a traditional school, where the academic day is split into multiple subject blocks, students at NuVu worked on a single project for a full two weeks and then moved on to another. By focusing on one project, students learned how to prioritize and manage their time. They also sought ways in which to take their learning forward. Coaches provided feedback in the early studios during the trimester, but as students learned how to formulate their own questions and critique their own work, coaches encouraged students to continuously reflect and see all the possibilities that might exist before asking for outside feedback as a way to push their ideas further.

At the end of every trimester, NuVu held an open innovation studio that allowed students who had advanced their creative and critical-thinking skills to pursue their own interests by pitching an idea for a project and framing the problem they were trying to solve. This process built on the skills that students had learned during the trimester and made a mental shift from responding to problems to identifying problems. This was vital within the studio process. It enabled students to extend what they had learned to areas of their personal interest, while retaining a critical mindset, even for those things that were most familiar to them.

An independent project period followed the open innovation studio where students had the choice to continue their work from a previous studio or from the open innovation studio, take on another student team's project to further develop it, or come up with a completely different project idea. This last studio in the trimester gave students more autonomy to work independently but still provided space for regular check-ins with coaches. Students felt a sense of mastery of the design process and were able to apply this process to their own problem.

Students have frequently continued work from their open innovation studio and independent project period outside of NuVu, demonstrating a continued pursuit of learning and passion for the projects they have initiated. NuVu has had a number of students pursue patents for their products and launch companies based around the ideas that students seeded at NuVu.

## Quest Program at Singapore American School

The Quest program, which Simon Bright, Darlene Poluan, and Katie Walthall engineered and led, gives twelfth-grade students at SAS almost complete agency over their learning experience. A full-time, year-round program, Quest gives students opportunities to demonstrate mastery of academic learning targets as well as desired student learning outcomes (DSLOs), such as communication, creativity, collaboration, critical thinking, character, and cultural competence.

From the onset, the Quest team sought to create a community of learners, starting first with teachers. Before the program even began, the three teachers, Bright, Poluan, and Walthall, came together fueled solely through their common belief in the potential to transform education. These teachers came from different disciplines and had various professional backgrounds and cultural influences. However, their common belief in reimagining education drove their work. The team members discovered that they had similar beliefs about what education should be: personalized, skills based, experiential, interdisciplinary, but mostly inspiring to students. This became the team mantra and guided future discussions.

Quest features six credits: (1) design thinking (science), (2) data analytics (mathematics), (3) research and composition (English), (4) cultural awareness and collaboration (social studies), (5) critical thinking and reasoning, and (6) creativity and innovation. To earn each credit, students had to demonstrate mastery of skills in a portfolio that documented their progress in various projects and through their interaction with the Quest advisors. The team identified forty-two different competencies that students could apply interchangeably for various projects that the facilitators and students would assess at least three times in the school year. Quest had students demonstrate mastery of essential disciplinary, transdisciplinary, and personalized learning outcomes through personalized learning pathways and personalized learning progressions. Student Voice: Quest features student experiences with the program.

### Student Voice: Quest

My name is Darlene, and I am a senior at the Singapore American School and a member of its inaugural Quest cohort. As a Quest member, I delivered my project purpose to parents and my classmates at a back-to-school-night presentation. Some of my teachers from last year also came by to watch my presentation. I loved the presentation because I was able to reflect on my experiences in Canada, and how much I learned a whole lot about myself. I talked about my strengths, preferences, collaboration skills, and interests and my goals for this year. Now that the presentation is over and I have my DSLOs, I can focus on the next semester!

This semester, we will be working on designing and creating effective classroom gadgets. Two weeks ago, we started our design thinking process; and last week, we got tutorials on how to work the 3-D-modeling software, the laser-cutter software, and other materials in the maker space. The advisors have invited guest coaches to assist us who are experts in computer programming, Arduino, and all kinds of electronic things. These electronics tutorials will hopefully give us a grounding to explore ways to use technology throughout the year. Since the theme is designing and creating effective classrooms, we had to identify the needs around the school, and then ideate, ideate, ideate! We brainstormed all kinds of things! At first, all twenty-four of us came up with ideas about what classroom gadgets could look like. Some thought they could be as simple as furniture and some came up with ideas as crazy as gadgets that will help teachers know what students are thinking! I wonder how they're going to create that! After the brainstorming process, we got into groups based on our interests in the brainstormed ideas. We are not allowed to work independently because designing requires collaboration.

I chose to work on the classroom furniture. We have several weeks to complete the project. We have to figure out how to research and gather knowledge about our project, contact and set up appointments with some teachers in the school to interview them about their use of classroom furniture, examine existing furniture to see the extent to which we can make it better, and so on. There is lots of work to do! On top of that, I still have research to do for my senior project. I don't know what I want to do for the entire year. I need to do some more self-reflection to determine what I would really like to focus on for the whole year. I'm glad the advisors are here for us. As much as I appreciate the flexibility, I really love that there is accountability.

## Collaboration

Collaboration is at the heart of Quest: collaboration between teachers, collaboration between teachers and students, and collaboration between students. The Quest community collaborated daily because it is a community of learners. Students even taught some skills and technical know-how. Advisors team-taught in Quest, so they discussed students' struggles and celebrated their successes regularly, and they also decided how to intervene in real time. There was constant personalized feedback for students. Quest also had an online portfolio that allowed each student to post artifacts about his or her projects and skills. Quest advisors observed the portfolios, sharing their collective perceptions, and assigned grades and interventions, posting comments to the various projects or artifacts. It was a fluid and continuous collaborative process.

Quest advisors attended scheduled, uninterrupted collaborative time every other day to catch up. This structure was similar to a traditional PLC collaborative team in that they discussed the students' progress collectively, decided on group interventions, and generally updated the other team members about some behind-the-scenes business of running the program. It was important to set aside uninterrupted time to really talk through any topics that may have been neglected or sensitive in the day-to-day education of students.

Much like some challenges that adults face when collaborating, significant issues arise when students collaborate. But if there is emotional safety in the group, advisors and students can deal with and overcome the issues. Sometimes there is a student or person who takes the lead, and because he or she seems to have it together, team members are happy to let him or her do all the work. Or there is a team member who leads through dominating and doesn't trust anyone else to do the work. The Quest team expected students to find a leadership style and to understand that leadership is about being not the bossiest person in the group, but rather the one who understands how to be authentic and deliver feedback that helps the team reach its goals. This required teams and individuals to value others' strengths. Many students struggled with feedback. Quest anticipated this issue, so the program took a group trip to the Canadian wilderness, where group members got to know and trust each other so they felt more comfortable. Quest also focused on helping students understand their strengths and other group members' strengths from the start of the year. This way, students understand, as they go through various group projects, the positive attributes they bring and others bring. These are concepts that the Quest team started teaching from the program's very beginning because of its belief in developing a community of learners and its desire to create students who can get along in any group and recognize the strengths and preferences of others.

# Critical Question 1: What Do I Want to Know, Understand, and Be Able to Do?

One major component of Quest is self-reflection and the pursuit of personal interests. Quest wants to inspire students to seek learning in its most authentic form, which is based on student curiosity and goal setting with these interests in mind. Quest students had some lofty goals, from getting strangers to play music together on the street to determining civic engineering that can help organize Syrian refugee camps. The students began setting learning targets that were far above their reach, and advisors helped break these learning targets down into small goals and put students in contact with experts who could help them achieve these goals.

In addition to identifying their learning targets, students would self-assess at the beginning of the year based on Quest standards. Students identified new information they needed for success on their senior project and determined learning targets through collaboration with peers, advisors, and experts in the field. All these would help them answer critical question 1 with confidence.

Table 9.1 shows how Quest transdisciplinary knowledge and skills relate to a traditional high school transcript and its subjects and grades. While the students are not taking individual classes in English, mathematics, science, and so on, they are demonstrating mastery of those content-area skills through their projects. The school notes the skills on the transcript so that colleges can see that students have completed the equivalent of AP English, data analytics (statistics), and so on.

TABLE 9.1: Quest Transcript

| Skills | Credits | Subjects |
|---|---|---|
| **Academic Skills** | 1.0 Advanced placement English: Research and composition | English |
| | 1.0 Advanced topic mathematics: Data analytics | Mathematics |
| | 1.0 Advanced topic science: Design thinking | Science |
| **DSLO Skills** | 1.0 Cultural awareness and collaboration | Social studies |
| | 1.0 Critical thinking and reasoning | Elective |
| | 1.0 Creativity and innovation | Elective |
| **Optional** | 1.0 Independent learning credit | Elective |

## Critical Question 2: How Will I Demonstrate That I Have Learned It?

Quest students must meet learning targets each unit while working on their senior project. However, the level of complexity and the various situations will affect mastery of learning. For example, one student was really creative in the arts, but not when working with a group to solve an issue with a service organization. She couldn't see at first how creativity could apply to solutions, until the ideation phase of the unit when she was coming up with really interesting solutions. One Quest advisor complimented her on her creativity, and that was when she realized that creativity was more than just being good at art. A student will know that he or she has mastered a target when he or she can demonstrate the ability to perform it multiple times during his or her senior year and in various contexts. However, mastery is never completely achieved; Quest emphasizes that everyone is constantly learning and wants students to understand that mastery is a process and to acknowledge learning when it takes place.

In order to accomplish this vision of proficiency, students will demonstrate proficiency of each standard three times in a year; self-advocate for their competency by adding artifacts to their portfolio; receive feedback from peers, advisors, and experts in the field to help determine that a learning target has been met; and engage in a self-reflection unit, which will allow students to reflect back and apply their skills in the future.

## Critical Question 3: What Will I Do When I Am Not Learning?

Quest students have ambitions that frequently lead them to encounter obstacles. The basic curriculum components (data analytics, design thinking, and research and composition) emphasize the acceptance of mistakes and inquiry to overcome obstacles. Learning is a quest. Quest called each student to do something great and relayed that there would be obstacles. Students didn't always know where they were going, or how they were going to get there, but there was always someone there to help along the way. The hero's journey metaphor of Quest emphasized the reality of learning. It rarely was done alone. It was never easy, and it was continuous. Advisors modeled this when freely admitting to something they didn't know how to do, and this helped students admit when they were stuck too. The first step was asking for help, and the second was knowing where to find it. The Quest community was a tight-knit group. Because they knew each other well, students and advisors continually learned from each other. Quest also frequently contacted experts in various academic fields and in various industries to help students. This sense of community and personalization of learning could help students when they were stuck and couldn't find the answer to regain their footing on the path to success.

So to answer critical question 3, students asked for help from peers, advisors, and community members; requested interventions from the Quest advisors when needed; were resourceful and learned how to conduct good research; and understood that they wouldn't develop skills in a day. Quest students had the opportunity to truly understand that perseverance, trial and error, and time are major factors in success.

## Critical Question 4: What Will I Do When I Have Already Learned It?

Quest's motto is "Time to be inspired." Quest gives students time to be inspired. This means that students chose a lot of what they wanted to work on within units—especially on the senior project. Many started with an idea based on something they already knew they were good at, and then they imagined extension possibilities. Students had the gift of time, and advisors were there to direct students to resources if they needed them, or to help them think about their projects from another perspective. How in depth a student went into a certain topic was as endless as the resources and his or her imagination. For example, in Quest, students who wanted to write a novel discovered what it is like to write a novel by actually writing a novel. They started with what they knew of writing, and then went beyond to discover new aspects, many that might have been unexpected. Quest believes there is no limit to what students can know and do if schools give them time to be inspired.

To create this ethos, students challenged themselves in a skill they were not as competent in, engaged in deeper exploration by testing and researching their assumption, moved on to a different project or chose to integrate more depth into their unit projects or senior projects, and gathered a team of expert students together to collaborate and pushed projects further.

# Project X at the International Community School of Addis Ababa

In the Horn of Africa lies an International Baccalaureate School that is attempting to give students a different level of agency over their learning. Project X is a program that gives high school sophomores the opportunity to identify and pursue their interests and passions by deliberately asking and answering the four critical questions of a PLC for themselves. Under high school principal David Redmond's leadership, this pilot program is giving students at the International Community School (ICS) of Addis

Ababa a different learning experience altogether. Project X uses personalized pathways to allow students to focus on transdisciplinary learning outcomes. This is Project X's story. See Student Voice: Project X for one student's experience.

## Collaboration

"OK, class—what do you want to learn this semester?" begins John Iglar, director of academic technology. The question shocks even those who knowingly signed up for the Project X course and have an end goal in mind. For others, Project X was simply a way to get out of another stultifying academic requirement, an elective with the potential to promise ample free time, little homework, and no testing. Most couldn't have imagined how over the next few months their initial surprise and wonder will morph into a vibrant and rewarding self-directed learning experience.

It is too rare to meet students who find sheer delight in the task of learning, but those who witness students' final presentations in Project X find a classroom full of them. Their projects are varied: a self-produced movie about the First World War, a dismantled and rebuilt desktop computer, a blog about astrophysics, and 3-D-printed models for a student-created computer game. Students create all of these products with their learning guided, but not provided, by their teacher. Mr. Iglar poses an initial question to serve as a launchpad for learning and guides the learning over a semester. Students brainstorm, plan, and revise their thinking—sometimes several times over the course of the project. Each student takes control over his or her own inquiry and determines the measures of his or her own success based on established criteria.

All students take an initial online course titled "Learning How to Learn," led by Barbara Oakley at University of California, San Diego. Over the four-week course, while students are acquiring tools and strategies for learning, they also, for the first time, begin to grapple with the big questions that educators have traditionally focused on: What do I want to learn? How do I know when I have learned it? What do I do when I get it? What do I do when I don't?

At the end of the semester, students present their learning to their peers, several teachers, and some parents. What's immediately noticeable is that a sense of efficacy pervades the group, and while everyone has had to confront his or her personal obstacles, there is no doubt about who is in control of the process and about who has taken ownership of the learning: the students. Remarkably, there is no shabby work on display; all students are proud of their products, and even if they haven't achieved their goals, they know why. Some leave the course with tasks to finish later, some have started new projects after realizing their initial goals more quickly than they had

## Student Voice: Project X

My name is Kristen. I am in grade 10. I think I am pretty well known to the entire school community for being an adventurous, hard-working, and committed learner. In both curricular and extracurricular pursuits, I bring a passion and zeal to all that I do. Like all of my friends, I am involved in a range of activities and carry a full course load of eight academic subjects, ranging from English, world languages, and social studies to science, arts, technology, and mathematics. I also participate in sports, drama, and volunteer my time for community service. I would call myself ambitious, but not driven by grades in the traditional sense as a student, so Project X's novel, individualized course of independent learning naturally appealed to me.

In Project X, students pursue an independent path of learning in an area of their choice. It need not be academic; it could be filmmaking or learning how to take apart a motherboard (to cite some student examples). The course facilitator guides us through the concepts and skills behind self-directed learning and helps us to develop a deeper understanding of our learning styles and how we can improve and expand our abilities to take charge of our own learning. We develop a personal learning plan and carry it out, reflecting on our learning throughout the process and in a reflective final self-assessment. Throughout the course, we meet with the teacher at regular checkpoints to review our progress and to consider the pathway forward.

As students in Project X, we collaborate with one another and with adults in a local and virtual community to locate learning opportunities and to build a network of support for the learning of our choice. For instance, some of my friends elected to take online courses, others pursued internships with mentors in the community, and others worked in traditional academic disciplines with teachers at the school. The Project X facilitator works to support us, providing guidance along the way.

The first step in our process is to decide on a path of learning. At the beginning, there is an almost overwhelming array of options and a keen sense of excitement. Here is an excerpt from my blog:

> *January 2016, a new year, a new beginning and definitely a cool new elective at ICS. Project X is an elective where we the students get to decide whatever we want to do!!!! Freedom—a word I never thought I would hear in school. We go to school and we're expected to learn certain things, nothing more. Our thirst for knowledge is buried under the stress of homework, and studying all the time. However, my school has given me the opportunity of a lifetime, to choose what I learn. I feel great!!! I haven't been this excited about an elective in our school for so long. I hope it meets all my expectations. I want to soak up so much knowledge this semester and explore so many ideas. I feel like there isn't enough time. I hope that I can effectively use my time and learn everything I want to sufficiently. Right now I have so many ideas about what I want to learn. I hope some reflection this weekend will help me make the best decision to help me improve my learning.*

anticipated, and others have changed course several times throughout the semester, moving among ideas until one finally resonated.

The presentations offer a brilliant demonstration of the excitement and passion to which a young person is susceptible when he or she is intrinsically motivated, and of what kinds of things happen when schools begin to think aspirationally about student outcomes, allowing students to drive the course. The students are in control and talk fluently about their learning. They are totally genuine and confident. It is amply evident that they hold what they know in a very deep place and that they are not presenting recycled facts or concepts they have little connection with. There is an individualization about their sense of ownership and agency that can be seen as the students talk about their projects. It is really impressive to witness their confidence in plain sight. For some of them, there is a sense that this is the first time that their learning experience has held weight and personal meaning, and that they have found delight in the task of learning. Try as we might, this is a place that the traditional teacher-centered classroom reaches infrequently.

## Critical Question 1: What Do I Want to Know, Understand, and Be Able to Do?

I (Kristen) have decided I want to learn more about law. I have many family members in this profession and it has always appealed to me, yet I am uncertain about it. I took the trial law course at ICS, and it was really great. We did a mock trial at the end, and I loved taking the role of the defense. But still I don't know if I should be putting all of my effort into tougher courses in order to prepare myself for law school or if I should maybe take more courses in science, too. I want to do the IB diploma, and I know that that will be very time-consuming, so I don't know if I will have any time for another course, even if it is an online law course. What if I change my mind? As a young Ethiopian woman, I feel that I need to go out and learn a profession and to someday give back to my country. I am also concerned about the gender imbalance of power in my country, let alone others, and I would like to do something to right this wrong. Maybe a career in law is the way to do this; maybe not. So, what I want to learn is about law, to get some experience with it by taking an online course and to see if this is really the path that I should be taking. By signing up for Project X, hopefully I can achieve my goal.

To learn more about law, I am taking an introductory course to become familiar with the topic. I want to have a solid and basic understanding of the fundamentals of law, its different types, how it works, and the big themes and ideas. I know I won't be able to become an expert overnight, but I want to have a command of the fundamentals.

## Critical Question 2: How Will I Demonstrate That I Have Learned It?

For my project, I want to create and write a law journal, article, or magazine (I haven't decided yet what format). I have decided this is the best way to demonstrate my learning for many reasons. First of all, I will have to write interesting articles about the subjects I have learned about, which will help me reinforce my learning and also share my knowledge with people who have no background in law. I am going to take an online course called "A Law Student's Toolkit" offered through Coursera by Yale University. It is designed to be taken over three weeks if you spend between five and seven hours a week at it. I don't know if I can fit that into my schedule, but I will try.

For the law course, I would like to invent something creative to show what I learn. I thought of putting together the art and the law course I want to learn and making it a creative and broad project that I will be able to display. I think I'm going to find it very interesting to mix up art and law and see what I am going to produce. I can't wait for it!

If I plan everything out now and create deadlines, everything will be in good order. I'm a very organized person, so I think that if I plan everything, I can pass most obstacles. Some problems I might face with being able to demonstrate my learning; however, I am working on a plan to overcome any obstacles.

I think that tests are not the best way to evaluate your knowledge; I believe other methods are more accurate. However, I do understand the purpose of tests; you must be able to demonstrate your knowledge. Otherwise, how can someone truly know that you've learned anything at all? What is the point of being knowledgeable about a certain subject if you can't share your knowledge with the rest of the world and help other people also gain that knowledge?

My final project will be my demonstration of just how much I have learned. I'm planning to write five articles and break down and teach people about some of the basics of law, but I also want to connect it to real life, so I will be sharing current and everyday examples that people can relate to. The artistic perspective will be the format, the pictures and the layout of the small journal. I'm planning to draw pictures to go along with the articles and also the magazine, so in this way, I will make it interesting and fun to read about law and also have an artistic side to my journal.

## Critical Question 3: What Will I Do When I Am Not Learning?

I must say my semester plans for the law course have definitely changed. I think my goals were a bit too unrealistic. The amount of content and assignments we had to complete for this course has taken more time than I expected, so I have moved my timeline. I plan on taking things a bit slower and my law course will finish about two weeks later than I planned, but that's okay. I would rather learn more over a longer time than speed through the course and not learn anything from it.

I'm a bit behind on my coursework. I have to work this weekend to finish unit four. I have struggled with understanding some of these concepts. I have decided to slow down and watch the videos multiple times and take time to absorb the information.

I have been working hard this spring break and past week to start my art course and create small pieces of art to help me with my final project. I have spent time exploring a variety of art; I drew people and intimate objects, did some shading and other intricate designs. The past two weeks of exploring art have been worthwhile. I have learned many new and efficient techniques that I will be employing in my final project.

## Critical Question 4: What Will I Do When I Have Already Learned It?

The techniques I learned from this course are invaluable. The techniques are helping me change my way of thinking and learning. I'm learning more quickly and efficiently, and I feel happier. I'm not dreading doing certain assignments anymore because I'm focused on not the product but rather the process. This course has really changed me as a student. Schoolwork is becoming easier and more manageable and procrastination is also slowly disappearing, so I can say Project X was one of the best things that has happened to me. The next thing for me to do is to talk to lawyers that I know and to get their advice on how I can continue my learning. I would like to take other online self-paced courses. I found out that if I commit myself to it, I can learn just about anything I want to.

# Senior Catalyst Program at Singapore American School

The senior catalyst program is a graduation requirement at SAS. It is a one-semester course designed to be a personalized learning pathway program for all seniors. The senior catalyst program at SAS under the leadership of Dennis Steigerwald and Bob Helmer offered high school students the opportunity to explore interests and pursue passions in new and flexible ways through a catalyst project. Each student conducted a self-study in order to initiate, develop, and complete an experiential project based on a topic of his or her choice. Teachers gave students agency over their learning and focused on personalizing instruction for each student and developing student skills of communication, collaboration, creativity, critical thinking, and cultural competence. The initial development for each semester project built on a preliminary student learning profile that students used to construct strategic and specific, measurable, attainable, results oriented, and time bound (or SMART; Conzemius & O'Neill, 2014) project goals. Students used a project framework to establish key learning targets, identified potential mentors, and requested personalized support from their teacher in order to help guarantee high levels of learning. In addition, students adopted project-management tools to help pace their work, ensure they completed a minimum viable product, and prepare them to present their learning journey to an authentic audience at the end of the semester. Throughout the project, mentors provided knowledge, insight, and experiences that would help students complete an authentic project while students and teachers provided critical friends feedback to enable constant reflection. A senior catalyst project allowed students to focus on essential transdisciplinary learning outcomes through a personalized learning pathways experience. Student Voice: Senior Catalyst Project features one student's experience.

### Student Voice: Senior Catalyst Project

My name is Janvi. I am a junior at Singapore American School. The catalyst course is currently an elective class, but will become a graduation requirement in a few years. I chose to take it because I wanted to explore ways to combine my academic interests with my personal interests.

The catalyst experience combines far more than my scheduled class time. All of my curricular, cocurricular, and extracurricular experiences earlier in my high school career help to set a foundation of knowledge, skills, and interests for me to launch into a catalyst project this year. For example, I have a number of friends who developed strong skills in computer science and coding while their experiences in app development, robotics, and design-engineering courses have sparked an interest in designing solutions for real-life technical issues. For my project, I designed, prototyped, and tested wearable technology that would monitor a person's body temperature and then send data to a responsive air conditioning system. My academic and coding background coupled with my experience in robotics provided the foundation for my project. My desire to combat the hot and humid conditions in Singapore helped motivate me to consider a project that integrated air conditioning systems with wearable technology. I would not have been able to complete such a complex catalyst project during one or two semesters of catalyst class time without a solid foundation of academic knowledge and skills.

continued ➡

I did not need to enter the catalyst program with a well-defined interest or idea. When I entered, I immediately put together a learning profile including strengths, interests, perceived needs, and potential constraints. This profile helped me construct an intrapersonal context in order to develop a rationale of why I might pursue a specific topic or type of project. If I had come to the class with a topic or project in mind, this exercise would have helped me reaffirm or reconsider my ideas. The learning profile sets the platform from which I can begin to immerse myself into exploring project themes and concepts. I started my catalyst project with a series of interests; yet I did not know what I wanted to specifically pursue. Once I had developed a learning profile identifying my strengths, interests, needs, and constraints, I was able to develop SMART goals that led me to explore a project based on wearable technology, coding, and improving a person's comfort.

My SMART goal also guides my project framework, mentorship, and management. Once I identified a topic of study based on my learning profile and goal, I began to frame my project and explore potential mentors from relevant professions and academic fields. Teachers help us focus on building our communication, collaboration, and networking skills since the program expects us to reach out, establish mentoring connections, and eventually complete a memorandum of understanding with a mentor. The mentors then begin to strengthen our framework of learning targets, experiences, and personalized support while teachers introduce us to project-management tools and strategies. At this point, we truly begin to direct and regulate our own learning while teachers and mentors act as "guides on the side." In my project, I was able to network and eventually establish a mentorship with a university professor who specialized in coding and technology. The mentor provided me with invaluable support in identifying what I needed to learn and be able to do, as well as providing resources, ideas, and sometimes viable solutions in order to successfully build a prototype of my wearable technology.

After my framework is complete and I have established mentorship, I move forward in developing a project-management plan based on completing a minimum viable product by the end of the semester. This plan includes a project goal, milestones with necessary subtasks to complete, due dates for completion, and specific checkpoints. For example, milestones for the wearable technology included initial research into the coding, hardware, and feasibility of wearable technology integrating with air conditioning. Once I found it was feasible, I created a series of prototypes and tested their ability to send signals to different air conditioning systems in order to provoke an automated response in temperature. Once I complete a minimum viable product, I will spend a few weeks preparing for my final project presentation where I am expected to present in front of an authentic audience that includes mentors, people from my established learning network, supportive teachers, my family members, friends, and other community members. I will be assessed not only on how I present, but on the focus of my topic, supporting evidence, organization, and overall effectiveness.

Throughout the entirety of the class, I receive peer and teacher feedback that I use to reflect about the process, my progress, struggles, and solutions; how I am progressing in finishing a minimum viable product for the class; and how well I am collaborating with peers and my mentor. I also receive feedback from teachers on my written work, progression of projects, and presentations. Instructors, volunteer parents, alumni, peers, and other students provide me with feedback using established skills-based rubrics and critical friends (peer review) protocols.

The catalyst program supported my interest in coding, integrating technologies, and solving the issue of unwanted temperature fluctuations within air-conditioned rooms. In addition, I was able to learn to be more entrepreneurial and feel better equipped to communicate and collaborate in college and eventually my career. Students also have the opportunity to complete an extended catalyst project—an SAS course designed for students like me who complete catalyst and want to get credit and support for continuing pursuit of passions. I have also been selected as an SAS Catalyst Fellow during my senior year, when I will be given even greater resources, time, and support to further pursue my interests and positively impact the world around me.

## Collaboration

Catalyst teachers and students collaborated around the four critical questions of a PLC. Teachers used the project framework to guide students in developing their own personalized learning targets based on the student's topic of interest. Collaboration in developing appropriate learning targets, networking resources, and real-world resources also occurred between mentors and students. In Janvi's story, his mentor provided expert guidance by pinpointing critical knowledge and skills Janvi needed to be able to develop wearable technology that monitored a person's vitals. He helped trouble-shoot circuitry issues to assist in making the system work, and he provided a network of experts that could help with identifying the correct infrared signals for communicating with air conditioners. While students got personalized instruction around their topics from their teachers, mentors provided invaluable knowledge and insight relevant to the projects' respective fields.

Also, students collaborated with each other through critical friends protocols so they got rapid feedback on their projects' progress and potential concerns while generating ideas that may help in future solutions. There was also goal-based collaboration at the projects' end, where students had to work in small groups to plan and execute their catalyst project presentations. Our student Janvi collaborated with three other students to work out how they would set up and break down their presentations, assist each other with technology and troubleshooting, and provide each other with moral support throughout the presentations. Theme-based collaboration is student generated and focuses on how students with similar interests have dialogue around a focused topic. This has included students working on a common-themed topic, such as developing a café in the high school or developing platforms and protocols for students to express themselves outside of normal classes.

## Critical Question 1: What Do I Want to Know, Understand, and Be Able to Do?

In the senior catalyst project, students developed strong self-awareness through building their learning profile and setting the goal of working with their mentor through their SMART goal. Students continued to outline what the program expected them to learn by developing a project canvas, a road map for their project. This canvas allowed students to answer the question of why do their project, flesh out essential components of the project, and figure out what the minimum viable product for their project would be. This work on the canvas laid the backbone for the later project framework where students developed ownership of their project and a strong sense of direction by focusing on a driving question and essential learning targets. Completion of these three essential class components provided students with a deep understanding of what teachers expected them to do and learn to complete the project.

## Critical Question 2: How Will I Demonstrate That I Have Learned It?

Teachers assessed students on their learning throughout the semester, first on their SMART goal. For Janvi, his SMART goal was to create a prototype device that connected the air conditioning in a room to a temperature gauge on someone in the room to allow the room's temperature to automatically adjust to the wearer's liking. Then, teachers assessed students on their framework, management plan, and portfolio artifacts using rubrics that aimed to gauge both the focus within the work and the details surrounding the work. The school assessed its DSLOs of critical thinking, collaboration, creativity, communication, cultural competence, character, and content knowledge through a series of benchmark portfolio submissions where each student had to submit an artifact demonstrating the DSLO, including completing a reflective rubric. In addition, students had to demonstrate their learning progress within their personalized learning targets through completing self-directed learning activities, apply what they had learned to their project, and then complete self-, peer-, and teacher-based assessments of their progress toward learning targets. An implicit assessment in many student projects came during prototyping and testing their product. When the student who created wearable technology created his first prototype, he encountered a very real-world assessment as he tested his comprehensive project for the first time. Thankfully, students often tested their products and their effectiveness well before they had to present their project at the semester's end. Ultimately, showcasing of their portfolio and their learning as a whole was the presentation project.

## Critical Question 3: What Will I Do When I Am Not Learning?

To ensure that students learned the DSLOs, they collaborated with other students using critical friends protocols four to five times during the semester. The feedback they got from their peers around their project as a whole and advice on overcoming challenges was essential to their learning. Also, their mentor could provide them with information, networking advice, and other opportunities to enhance their learning. Individually, students had the opportunity to fail and keep moving forward in their project. The school expected them to conduct observations, develop a network, collect data, and experiment with and prototype their work to demonstrate their curiosity and inquisitiveness. Teachers conducted regular checkpoint interviews with students where teachers identified them as being either *green*, or fully on track and ready for more freedom in their learning; *yellow*, or cautionary, where the teacher will continue to monitor student progress; or *red*, or falling behind and needing close monitoring and support in their next steps.

Throughout the project, students were self-directed by their own project-management plan to learn specific topics and complete tasks that oriented themselves toward the milestone accomplishments necessary in order to complete the project. When challenges occurred, and they always did, students had to problem-solve and modify their plans accordingly. Routinely, teachers required students to provide written observations of their challenges, collect feedback from students, and then reflect on their progress, attempted solutions, and next steps. Our student Janvi reflected on the fact that he had originally struggled with the coding behind his devices but was able to ask questions of his network, including computer science teachers, his mentor, mentor associates, and other students, to overcome these difficulties, and conduct further investigation into the debugging of the code to solve the issues.

## Critical Question 4: What Will I Do When I Have Already Learned It?

Finally, for students who already had the skills the program cultivated, teachers deemed their work self-directed, and they got the green light to continue on their own. A good project is never truly done. Our student Janvi continued to work on his air conditioning body temperature device throughout the summer and took an extended catalyst class in the fall of his senior year. Students could continue to work on their project during this extended catalyst class or dive deeper into aspects of their project by taking a hyper-catalyst class during a subsequent semester. A hyper-catalyst experience is an unprecedented opportunity for students to receive exceptional time, resources, and support to complete projects during school time yet outside the normal constructs of day-to-day classroom instruction. Once again, students could continue to build on their learning and strengths profile, as well as further develop a professional network and link their work into the future. The major scaffolding of the class's flow—framing learning with SMART goals, having mentor networking, engaging in project management, developing a portfolio of work, showcasing the work, and consistently giving and receiving feedback—were all areas that students could dive deeper into and further develop.

High schools are often the most reluctant to introduce personalized learning experiences for their students. The schedule, advanced precollege courses, and the fear of creating what could be perceived to be a nonrigorous experience seem to be common roadblocks. The schools featured in this chapter are considered some of the most academically rigorous in the world. They have found that it is these personalized learning programs that allow their most gifted students to apply their learning at a whole new level and give them a distinguishing factor when applying to selective colleges.

### Questions to Consider

Consider the following four questions as you begin your transformation to a highly effective and learning-progressive school.

1. **The learning:** What are the important learnings for me in this chapter? For my school? What am I inspired to know and be able to do?

2. **The evidence:** What are we already doing that aligns with this paradigm? What would change in my school and professional experience if we further embrace and implement it?

3. **The learning pit:** What obstacles would we face if we were to try or to further this approach? What strategies could we use to experience breakthroughs?

4. **The lever:** What would we need to accelerate the change process?

# PART FOUR

# Committing to Change

# 10

# The Change Process and Strategic Planning

In their book *The Global Fourth Way*, Andy Hargreaves and Dennis Shirley (2012) suggest that schools must "harmonize incremental improvements with disruptive change . . . to develop innovation within schools while continuously improving them" (p. 27). It is important for schools to find the balance between these two change processes. This is particularly true for high-performing schools. If creating a culture of disruptive innovation kills our thirst for continuous improvement, we run the risk of having no substance underneath the veneer. Schools need to find ways to create disruptive change and revolutionize education through building on the structures that made them great in the first place. It is for this reason that we are strongly advocating building on the PLC model as the foundation to become a highly effective and learning-progressive school. In this chapter, we explore the change process as it happened at SAS, including change leadership, the research and development process, and strategic planning.

## Change Leadership

One thing to consider in the change process is speed. How fast do we go to ensure that change happens? How do we know when we are going too fast or too slow?

Implementing change is like pushing a car up a hill. If you take a running start and hit the car (even if you hit it hard), it's not going to budge. You have to apply consistent pressure in the same direction in order to get the car to start moving. Once the car is moving, you can increase its speed. Even if you need to take a breather (and we all do from time to time), you still need to keep some amount of pressure on the car, or the car will start rolling down the hill in the opposite direction. During one of our visits to High Tech High in San Diego, its CEO and founding principal Larry Rosenstock suggested that the number-one challenge with the change process is to fight the inertia and tendency to "regress toward the mean"—in other words, roll back down the hill (L. Rosenstock, personal communication, October 2014). Change is hard, very hard, particularly if what we are trying to change connects to what teachers hold dearest— students' learning outcomes. It often feels as if everything in the system rallies to keep the status quo in place. Our natural temptation is to keep answering the first PLC critical question—What do we want all students to know and be able to do?—the same way we always have. Answering it differently means changes, which can be very difficult.

How will you know when you are pushing too hard for change, or not hard enough? You use common sense! Know the people you are working with. Understand their capacity and appetite for change. As Michael Fullan (2011) puts it, the first "secret of change" is to "love your employees" (p. 19). Love them enough so that they trust you enough to believe you when you say that this change is worthwhile. Love them enough to admit when you've made a wrong decision and you need to reconsider things. Love them enough to know when you are pushing them too hard. Love and know them enough to know when you are not pushing hard enough.

Unfortunately, however, love is *not* enough. John P. Kotter (2012) suggests that the first step for initiating systemic change is to "establish a sense of urgency" (p. 37). Yes, knowing your team and creating a culture of mutual trust and responsibility are absolutely imperative to change, but your community must also understand the *why*. Why is it important for the community to embark down this difficult road? Is this work going to really make a difference for students and their learning? The why is not only important to establish at the beginning of the change process; change leaders must regularly come back to the why and continuously remind the community why it is doing this, why it is important to do this, and what will happen to the school and students if the community doesn't.

Not all of us have the advantage of having the Nokia headquarters in our driveway, like the highly successful secondary school we visited in Finland. We must establish our own Nokia, our own sense of urgency.

The following section describes a stage-by-stage model of change. This is not a formula for successful change. These are simply the steps that one school, the Singapore American School, took in order to make significant changes in its community—steps that ultimately culminated in the school changing its answer to critical question 1 and giving its students increased agency over their learning using the PLC model.

# The Research and Development Process

Under the leadership of its superintendent, Chip Kimball, SAS established a comprehensive research and development process to achieve its vision to be a world leader in education, cultivating exceptional thinkers prepared for the future. The school developed a four-stage process to manage the transformational process thoughtfully and to ensure maximum success and sustainability of new programs.

The four stages that follow—(1) research and anchors, (2) development, (3) capacity building, and (4) implementation and strategic planning—draw on the Singapore American School process. You can use these at a district level, a school level, or a collaborative team level. While we recognize that the spark it requires for change can often come from an individual innovative teacher, we suggest that a thoughtful change process is most effective and salable if done within the context of a collaborative team.

## Research and Anchors

The research and anchors stage gives teachers and administrators a designated amount of time to dive deep into the educational literature and learn from other schools in their region or around the world. It is important to choose schools that are doing things differently and will challenge your thinking and practice. A great framework to use for choosing schools to visit is whether a school has a reputation of being both highly effective *and* learning progressive. These are schools on the cutting edge of teaching and learning.

During stage 1, Singapore American School teachers and administrators visited over one hundred schools in seven countries. The article "Creating the Future of Learning: Singapore American School" (Getting Smart staff, 2016) suggests:

> [Singapore American School] used school visits to inspire a talented but isolated faculty. Exposure to the best schools in the world and a new group of critical friends resulted in updated student learning expectations. Professional learning communities created collaboration routines that broke down barriers and hosted tough conversations. New tools created new learning opportunities. (p. 15)

The primary objective during the research and anchors stage is simply to learn. As educators, we love learning, but sometimes we don't "get out enough." SAS learned from thought leaders in the field and from schools around the world. Staff learned from exemplar schools, but also from schools yet to begin their change process. Teams reported that their learning from stagnant schools was equally indelible.

The second objective of the research and anchors stage is to create a sense of urgency for teachers and administrators. Seeing the extent to which students can empower their own learning shone a spotlight on traditional practices and left the team feeling dissatisfied with the status quo and hungry for change.

Last but not least, the third objective for SAS was to ask itself these questions: "What are the learning outcomes we want our students to master?" "What instructional approach will help our students become proficient in those learning outcomes?" "What do we want to be known for?" "What is going to set us apart from other schools?"

At the end of a year of research, school visits, and a lot of soul-searching, SAS identified three cultures it wanted to embody. Staff noticed that many of the top-performing schools in the world could claim one or two of these cultures, but only a handful could claim to embrace all three: (1) a culture of excellence, (2) a culture of extraordinary care, and (3) a culture of possibilities.

1. **Culture of excellence:** Every student learns at high levels.

2. **Culture of extraordinary care:** Every student is known and advocated for.

3. **Culture of possibilities:** Every student personalizes his or her learning.

Figure 10.1 represents what became known as the SAS strategic anchors: the three cultures that it wanted to uniquely define who it is as a school. Its staff believe that the sweet spot of learning is at the intersection of each of these cultures. These disciplinary and transdisciplinary learning outcomes of critical thinking, creativity, communication, collaboration, cultural competence, character, and content knowledge (called DSLOs) became more defined and clarified. SAS believes that deep learning of the DSLOs happens when extraordinary care, an expectation for excellence, and a culture of possibilities intersect. From this point on, all of SAS's strategic decisions would be vetted through this lens. It considers and applies all SAS strategic anchors in all decision making. The following strategic anchors represent the cultural norms of the school.

## Development

The development stage gives teacher teams the opportunity to make sense of all the research and to devise a school-reform proposal from their research. It is important to put everything on the table during this stage, be willing to sacrifice traditions, and ask the hard questions. If we were to design a new school today, what would it look like? Given everything that we have read and seen, what can we implement that would positively and dramatically impact student learning in our school? Asking and answering

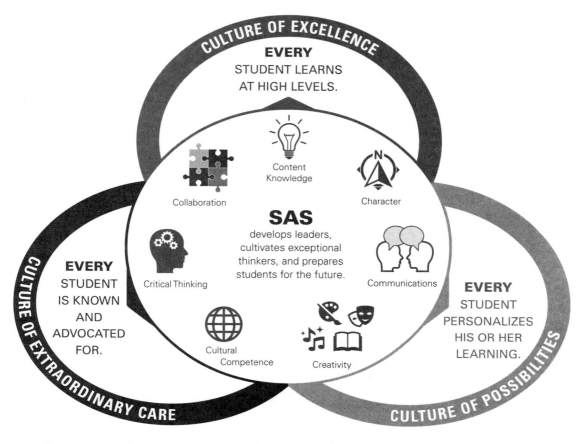

*Source: © 2016 by Singapore American School. Reprinted with permission.*

**Figure 10.1:** The SAS strategic anchors.

these questions will be difficult and often emotional, getting at the heart of what we hold dearest as teachers: the way we do things now.

High-performing schools aren't forged accidentally. They are forged because well-intentioned, hardworking, and passionate educators have spent years shaping them to be what they are. Naturally, the threat of deconstructing things will be met with caution, if not outright opposition. That is valid and understandable because people believe in what they have built.

To navigate these waters successfully, it's important to keep the early conversations at a pretty high level—the thirty-thousand-foot conversation. It's easier for team members to come to an agreement on some big ideas first and then move to more specific implications. For example, the team agrees that students who can exercise agency over their learning are more successful than students who don't own their learning. The next step would be to decide how the team or school is going to give students the opportunity to own their learning process.

## Capacity Building

Once the team or school endorses or establishes a set of recommendations, it is imperative to carve out time to implement each initiative well so teachers can lead and participate. The capacity-building stage allows each team or school to bolster itself to implement plans with fidelity and excellence. This stage includes professional development, piloting and prototypes, and new course development.

Ultimately, our desire should be to move the team or organization forward without negatively impacting the students' learning experience. It has been our observation that many teams or schools jump right into implementation without giving enough time and support to develop the organization's capacity to deliver. This is a classic mistake that can all too often create a false start or derail the initiative altogether.

It is during this stage that the school or team should establish and execute a robust stakeholder communication plan. It is impossible to over-communicate during a change process.

## Implementation and Strategic Planning

Once the team or school has built its capacity, it enters into the implementation phase. If the change is happening at a team level, the change is a lot simpler and can be done relatively quickly. If the recommended changes are at a schoolwide level, stage 4 requires the school to prioritize initiatives and how it will roll them out over a one- to five-year time frame. The school must gauge its capacity to implement change considering several factors, including schoolwide alignment, the initiative's importance, if there are things that need to be addressed first, and the school's climate and appetite for change.

Table 10.1 provides an overview of the research and development stages.

**TABLE 10.1: The Four Research and Development Stages**

| Stage | Description |
|---|---|
| **Stage 1:** **Research and Anchors** | Teams dive deep into the educational literature around learning and visit highly effective and learning-progressive schools. |
| **Stage 2:** **Development** | Teams use their research and school visits to develop a reform proposal. |
| **Stage 3:** **Capacity Building** | Teams build capacity through professional development to implement the plan successfully. |
| **Stage 4:** **Implementation and Strategic Planning** | The team or school carefully and thoughtfully rolls out the initiative based on the team or organization's priorities and capacity. (While the first three stages are team based, stage 4 must be implemented at the school level. This ensures that all new programs align with the entire school's mission and vision.) |

# The Strategic Plan

The strategic plan outlines a six-year plan to move an entire school from its current iteration to a desired future. Singapore American School identifies five strategic areas of focus: (1) PLCs, (2) a standards-based approach, (3) high-impact instructional practices, (4) pastoral care, and (5) systems supporting learning (see figure 10.2, page 176).

The power of a well-crafted strategic plan is to help the organization focus on the most important areas—the things that will yield the highest return on a school's investment. For SAS, PLC continues to be its top priority even after five years of implementation, not because of some external mandate, but because it continues to experience the impact that PLC is having on student learning each and every day.

Let's unpack the first strategic area. For the purposes of this book, we will only unpack this strategic area since this is the one that focuses on PLCs. Remember, this strategic area aims to move SAS forward. To this end, you will notice that PLCs are learning organisms. They help us improve our instructional approach to best meet students' ever-changing needs. As we have articulated throughout this book, in order to help students take ownership of their learning and personalize their learning progression and pathways, PLCs must move from teachers having primary agency in the learning of students, to students having agency over their learning.

The strategic plan identifies PLCs as teachers actively engaging in effective teams whose members work interdependently to achieve common student learning goals for which members are mutually accountable.

# Purpose of PLC at SAS

We believe every student has value and can learn at high levels. PLCs guarantee a common, viable curriculum where teams take collective responsibility for all students' learning. PLCs ensure that faculty work collaboratively to leverage their expertise and analyze evidence of learning to improve their own practice and maximize each student's learning and growth.

## Guiding PLC Principles at SAS

The strategic plan identifies the guiding PLC principles as follows.

- Collaborative teams focus on and commit to the learning of each student.

- Collaborative teams focus on collective learning for *all* (students and teachers).

| Professional Learning Communities | Standards-Based Approach | High-Impact Instructional Practices | Pastoral Care |
|---|---|---|---|
| PLCs focus on learning. | Assessments target essential learning outcomes at macro (unit) and micro (learning progression) levels. | Staff use high-impact practices to explicitly teach the DSLOs. | A culture of extraordinary care that supports students exists. |
| PLCs commit to continuous improvement by collectively focusing on results. | Evidence of student learning is gathered for each DSLO. | Students regularly engage in inquiry to deepen learning. | Social-emotional programs exist to help students develop social and emotional wellness. |
| PLCs collectively answer the four critical questions and apply those answers to their individual contexts. | Assessments are valid, reliable, and fair. | Students engage in experiential learning opportunities, including service learning. | Advisory programs exist to ensure every student is known, connected, and cared for. |
| Structures exist, and staff use them to support intervention and extension. | Evaluation (grading) and reporting of student learning are standards based. | Practices and programs allow for personalization of learning. | Students are supported through major transitions (new to SAS, exiting SAS, and between divisions). |
| Structures exist, and staff use them to support effective PLC collaboration. | Structures exist, and staff use them to support a standards-based approach. | Structures exist, and staff use them to support high-impact instructional practices. | Structures exist, and staff use them to support pastoral care. |

**Systems Supporting Learning**

With service excellence as a lens, preK–12 departments collaborate to create and improve effective and integrated schoolwide systems to ensure adults have the capacity to support students and learning.

*Source: © 2016 by Singapore American School. Reprinted with permission.*

**Figure 10.2:** SAS strategic areas of focus.

- Collaborative teams work through an ongoing recurring cycle of collective inquiry and action research to achieve better results for the students they serve.

- Collaborative teams are action oriented; they move quickly to turn aspirations into action and visions into reality.

- Collaborative teams center themselves on data and evidence of learning instead of intentions.

- Collaborative teams answer the following four critical questions (DuFour et al., 2016):

  a. What is it that we want students to know, understand, and be able to do?

  b. How will we know if they learn it?

  c. How will we respond when some students do not learn?

  d. How will we extend the learning for students who are already proficient?

### Success Indicator Rubric at SAS

Singapore American School uses the rubric in figure 10.3 (page 178) to monitor its success in realizing its strategic plan. The Applying column of this rubric represents what is currently considered PLC best practices. The implementation of PLCs with fidelity is an essential step in this process. As we've said earlier, it is impossible to become high-performing and learning-progressive schools without creating a strong foundation from which to launch. We fundamentally believe that the PLC framework provides the best foundation for this work.

The Innovating column of this rubric gives direction to the work ahead. It helps articulate and then hold teams accountable to a preferred future. This aspirational column creates a set of standards against which teams can measure their journey, a journey that leads to student agency of their learning process. The clear message here is that engaging students in the PLC learning process is part of the PLC continuum. Bringing students into the collective responsibility of learning and giving them agency of their learning are not separate from a PLC. This is not a new initiative. It is the actualization of the PLC process. Bold text under the Professional Learning Communities Strategic Plan Rubric row indicates aspirational goals for SAS's teams.

## Rubric Levels

| Developing | Applying | Innovating |
|---|---|---|
| The following occurs at this level. <br><br> • Implementation of strategy occurs without significant error. <br> • Consistency of process is still in progress. <br> • No monitoring of impact on student learning occurs. | The following occurs at this level. <br><br> • Strategy reflects the currently stated goal. <br> • There is strategy implementation without errors and with relative ease. <br> • Consistency of process exists. <br> • Teams monitor impact on student learning. | The following occurs at this level. <br><br> • Strategy reflects the strategic goal. <br> • Teams adapt the strategy to meet specific student needs. <br> • Students engage with and own the strategy. |

## Professional Learning Communities Strategic Plan Rubric

| Standard | Developing | Applying | Innovating |
|---|---|---|---|
| 1.1: Teams focus on learning. | Teams share a common understanding of learning and the learning process. Members believe that all students can learn at high levels but are inconsistent in demonstrating a growth mindset. | Teams utilize a common understanding of learning and the learning process. Team members believe that all students can learn at high levels and demonstrate a growth mindset. | Students understand the learning process and are able to utilize it to describe where they are in their learning. Students apply a growth mindset to themselves and take responsibility to promote their own learning. |
| 1.2: Teams commit to continuous improvement and focus on results through achieving common goals. | Teams gather evidence of student learning and use the results to respond to individual student needs, improve professional practice, or both. | Teams frequently gather evidence of student learning, formulate SMART goals to guide their team in taking purposeful action, and use the results to respond to individual student needs, improve professional practice, and analyze the impact of changes they are making. | Students frequently gather evidence of their learning and develop SMART goals to guide themselves in taking purposeful action. |

| | | | |
|---|---|---|---|
| 1.3: Teams collectively answer the four PLC questions and apply those answers to their individual classrooms. | Teams clarify essential knowledge and skills for each unit of study and agree to common summative and formative assessments to use in assessing the quality of student work. They identify students who need intervention or extension and develop appropriate support. Not all team members apply the answers to the PLC questions in their individual classrooms. | Teams clarify essential knowledge and skills for each unit of study and agree to common summative and formative assessments to use in assessing the degree to which students demonstrate proficiency. They identify students who need intervention, extension, or both, and develop appropriate support. Each team member applies the answers to the PLC questions in his or her individual classroom. | Students are able to articulate what teachers expect them to do to demonstrate proficiency and where they are in relation to the target. They are able to utilize strategies to help themselves when they are struggling and to extend themselves when they have already demonstrated proficiency. |
| 1.4: Teams use existing structures to support intervention and extension to ensure high levels of learning for all students. | Teams recognize that the success of each student is the collective responsibility of all team members. Teams utilize pyramids of intervention or acceleration as they need to. Teams struggle to adhere to guidelines for moving students from Tier 1 to Tier 2 to Tier 3; instead they heavily rely on Tier 3 intervention. | There is a widely held belief that the success of each student is the collective responsibility of all team members. Teams utilize pyramids of intervention and acceleration as they need to. Teams adhere to guidelines for moving students from Tier 1 to Tier 2 to Tier 3, relying on Tier 3 intervention only after trying and monitoring other strategies. | |

**Figure 10.3:** Strategic plan monitoring tool.

Our intention for this chapter is not to elevate one particular school as a flawless model for change; it is simply a process that we are intimately connected to. The Singapore American School has chosen to use the PLC model to create personalized learning experiences for its students. Its desire to become a highly effective learning-progressive school only reinforced its commitment to its fundamental beliefs as a PLC. In many ways, SAS answers the question of whether being a PLC and being an innovative school are mutually exclusive. SAS's answer is clear: absolutely not! In fact, it is SAS's belief that without the PLC construct, innovative programs can't be progressive and effective.

## Rate Your Progression

What are the specific factors in your school environment that contribute to a sense of urgency for change?

## Tips for Transformation

The following are three tips to transform school culture.

1. **Find ways to create disruptive change and revolutionize education:** Schools build on the structures that made them great in the first place to accomplish this.

2. **Use the PLC process:** Schools should build on the PLC process as the foundation to become a highly effective and learning-progressive school.

3. **Follow the four-stage process:** Schools need the four-stage change process to manage the transformational process thoughtfully and to ensure maximum success and sustainability of new programs: (1) research and anchors, (2) development, (3) capacity building, and (4) implementation.

**?**

## Questions to Consider

Consider the following four questions as you begin your transformation to a highly effective and learning-progressive school.

1. **The learning:** What are the important learnings for me in this chapter? For my school? What am I inspired to know and be able to do?

2. **The evidence:** What are we already doing that aligns with this paradigm? What would change in my school and professional experience if we further embrace and implement it?

3. **The learning pit:** What obstacles would we face if we were to try or to further this approach? What strategies could we use to experience breakthroughs?

4. **The lever:** What would we need to accelerate the change process?

# Epilogue

Change in schools is hard and complex, particularly when it involves changing what we believe students should know and be able to do. It requires foresight, strategy, patience, and, above all, courage—courage to do what we know is right for the students we serve.

We know more today about how to facilitate learning at high levels and what is truly important for children to learn than ever before, but many schools are simply not changing the learning experience. The time to change is now. Our hope is that this book will reinforce the sense of urgency and present compelling reasons to begin the change process and give educators a simple yet research-based and reliable construct to provide students with increased agency over and personalization of their learning.

In the end, what matters most is providing students with learning environments that foster high levels of learning and engagement for all students. By bringing students into the PLC conversation, we can truly give students the ability to take concrete and measurable steps to increase their learning.

Finally, we are absolutely convinced that while change is hard and complex, it is made significantly more doable and sustainable in a high-functioning PLC. Any school contemplating beginning this transformational journey should begin by becoming a PLC. This proven construct will create the learning-focused culture that is necessary to truly give students agency and allow them to own their learning and learn at the highest level.

# References and Resources

Agency (philosophy). (n.d.). In *Wikipedia*. Accessed at https://en.wikipedia.org/wiki/Agency_(philosophy) on October 12, 2017.

Bandura, A. (1994). Self-efficacy theory. In V. S. Ramachaudran (Ed.), *Encyclopedia of human behavior* (Vol. 4, pp. 71–81). New York: Academic Press. (Reprinted in H. Friedman [Ed.], *Encyclopedia of mental health*. San Diego: Academic Press, 1998).

Barber, M., Chijioke, C., & Mourshed, M. (2010). *How the world's most improved school systems keep getting better*. Accessed at www.mckinsey.com/industries/social-sector/our-insights/how-the-worlds-most-improved-school-systems-keep-getting-better on February 24, 2017.

Barber, M., & Mourshed, M. (2007). *How the world's best-performing schools come out on top*. Accessed at http://mckinseyonsociety.com/how-the-worlds-best-performing-schools-come-out-on-top on February 24, 2017.

Bartlett, J. (1919). *Familiar quotations: A collection of passages, phrases, and proverbs traced to their sources in ancient and modern literature*. Boston: Little, Brown, and Company.

Boaler, J., Chen, L., Williams, C., & Cordero, M. (2016). Seeing as understanding: The importance of visual mathematics for our brain and learning. *Journal of Applied Computational Mathematics, 5*(325). Accessed at www.omicsonline.org/peer-reviewed/seeing-as-understanding-the-importance-of-visual-mathematics-for-our-brain-and-learning-80807.html on March 3, 2018.

Buffum, A., Mattos, M., & Malone, J. (2018). *Taking action: A handbook for RTI at Work*. Bloomington, IN: Solution Tree Press.

Buffum, A., Mattos, M., & Weber, C. (2012). *Simplifying response to intervention: Four essential guiding principles*. Bloomington, IN: Solution Tree Press.

Conzemius, A. E., & O'Neill, J. (2014). *The handbook for SMART school teams: Revitalizing best practices for collaboration* (2nd ed.). Bloomington, IN: Solution Tree Press.

Costa, A. L., & Kallick, B. (2014). *Dispositions: Reframing teaching and learning.* (1st ed.). Thousand Oaks, CA: Corwin.

Daggett, W. R. (2004). *America's most successful high schools: Case studies and resources on best practices.* Rexford, NY: International Center for Leadership in Education.

Dewey, J. (1897). My pedagogic creed. *School Journal, LIV*(3), 77–80.

Dewey, J. (1938). *Experience & education.* Indianapolis, IN: Kappa Delta Pi.

Duckworth, A. (2016). *Grit: The power of passion and perseverance.* New York: Scribner.

DuFour, R. (2015). *In praise of American educators: And how they can become even better.* Bloomington, IN: Solution Tree Press.

DuFour, R. (2016). *Advocates for professional learning communities: Finding common ground in education reform.* Accessed at www.allthingsplc.info/files/uploads /AdvocatesforPLCs-Updated11-9-15.pdf on February 27, 2017.

DuFour, R., DuFour, R., & Eaker, R. (2008). *Revisiting Professional Learning Communities at Work: New insights for improving schools.* Bloomington, IN: Solution Tree Press.

DuFour, R., DuFour, R., Eaker, R., & Many, T. W. (2006). *Learning by doing: A handbook for Professional Learning Communities at Work.* Bloomington, IN: Solution Tree Press.

DuFour, R., DuFour, R., Eaker, R., Many, T. W., & Mattos, M. (2016). *Learning by doing: A handbook for Professional Learning Communities at Work* (3rd ed.). Bloomington, IN: Solution Tree Press.

DuFour, R., & Eaker, R. (1998). *Professional Learning Communities at Work: Best practices for enhancing student achievement.* Bloomington, IN: Solution Tree Press.

DuFour, R., & Fullan, M. (2013). *Cultures built to last: Systemic PLCs at Work.* Bloomington, IN: Solution Tree Press.

DuFour, R., & Marzano, R. J. (2011). *Leaders of learning: How district, school, and classroom leaders improve student achievement.* Bloomington, IN: Solution Tree Press.

DuFour, R., Reeves, D., & DuFour, R. (2018). *Responding to the Every Student Succeeds Act with the PLC at Work process.* Bloomington, IN: Solution Tree Press.

Dweck, C. S. (2006). *Mindset: The new psychology of success.* New York: Random House.

European Parliament, Council of the European Union. (2006, December 18). *Recommendation of the European Parliament and of the Council on key competencies for lifelong learning.* Accessed at http://eur-lex.europa.eu/legal-content/EN/ALL /?uri=celex%3A32006H0962 on October 12, 2017.

Farrington, C. A., Roderick, M., Allensworth, E., Nagaoka, J., Keyes, T. S., Johnson, D. W., & Beechum, N. O. (2012). *Teaching adolescents to become learners: The role of noncognitive factors in shaping school performance—A critical literature review.* Chicago: University of Chicago Consortium on Chicago School Research.

Ferguson, R. F. (2015). *The influence of teaching: Beyond standardized test scores—Engagement, mindsets, and agency: A study of 16,000 sixth through ninth grade classrooms.* Cambridge, MA: The Achievement Gap Initiative at Harvard University.

Fleer, M., Edwards, S. E., Hammer, M. D., Kennedy, A. M., Ridgeway, A., Robbins, J. R., & Surman, L. W. (2006). *Early childhood learning communities. Sociocultural research in practice.* (1st ed.) Melbourne, Australia: Pearson.

Fullan, M. (2011). *The six secrets of change: What the best leaders do to help their organizations survive and thrive.* San Francisco: Jossey-Bass.

Fullan, M., & Langworthy, M. (2014). *A rich seam: How new pedagogies find deep learning.* London: Pearson. Accessed at www.michaelfullan.ca/wp-content/uploads/2014/01/3897.Rich_Seam_web.pdf on October 13, 2015.

Garmston, R., & Wellman, B. (1999). *The adaptive school: A sourcebook for developing collaborative groups.* Norwood, MA: Christopher-Gordon.

Getting Smart staff. (2016). *Creating the future of learning: Singapore American School.* Accessed at www.gettingsmart.com/wp-content/uploads/2016/05/Singapore-American-School.pdf on January 8, 2018.

Hargreaves, A., & Shirley, D. (2012). *The global fourth way: The quest for educational excellence.* Thousand Oaks, CA: Corwin Press.

Hattie, J. (2008). *Visible learning: A synthesis of over 800 meta-analyses relating to achievement* [Kindle version]. Didcot, England: Taylor & Francis.

Hattie, J. (2009). *Visible learning: A synthesis of over 800 meta-analyses relating to achievement.* New York: Routledge.

Hattie, J. (2012). *Visible learning for teachers: Maximizing impact on learning.* New York: Routledge.

Hattie, J. (2014). *Hattie ranking: 195 influences and effect sizes related to student achievement.* Accessed at http://visible-learning.org/hattie-ranking-influences-effect-sizes-learning-achievement on October 13, 2015.

Hattie, J. (2016, July 11). *Mindframes and maximizers.* Third Annual Visible Learning Conference, Washington, DC.

Hitlin, S., & Elder, G. H., Jr. (2007). Time, self, and the curiously abstract concept of agency. *Sociological Theory, 25*(2), 170–191.

Hoffer, E. (2006). *Reflections of the human condition.* Titusville, NJ: Hopewell.

Institute for the Future. (2007, October). *The future of work: Perspectives.* Accessed at www.iftf.org/uploads/media/SR%201092-A_FoWPerspectives_screen.pdf on October 12, 2017.

Jawabra, Z. (2016, March 1). *Nokia CEO ended his speech saying this "we didn't do anything wrong, but somehow, we lost"* [Blog post]. Accepted at http://artserv.blogspot.com/2016/03/nokia-ceo-ended-his-speech-saying-this.html on October 12, 2017.

Jerald, C. D. (2009). *Defining a 21st century education.* Alexandria, VA: Center for Public Education.

Kelley, T., & Littman, J. (2007). *The art of innovation: Lessons in creativity from IDEO, America's leading design firm.* New York: Crown Business.

Kirschner, P., & Van Merriënboer, J. J. G. (2008). *Ten steps to complex learning: A new approach to instruction and instructional design.* Accessed at https://pdfs .semanticscholar.org/8972/359c6b192ab479e81416cd725918babf4df4.pdf on December 20, 2017.

Kotter, J. P. (2012). *Leading change, with a new preface by the author.* Boston: Harvard Business School Press.

Lai, E. R., DiCerbo, K. E., & Foltz, P. (2017). *Skills for today: What we know about teaching and assessing collaboration.* London: Pearson.

Lezotte, L. W. (2005). More effective schools: Professional learning communities in action. In R. DuFour, R. Eaker, & R. DuFour (Eds.), *On common ground: The power of professional learning communities* (pp. 177–191). Bloomington, IN: Solution Tree Press.

Malaguzzi, L. (1993). History, ideas, and basic philosophy. In C. Edwards, L. Gandini, & G. Forman, *The Hundred Languages of Children: The Reggio Emilia Approach To Early Childhood Education.* Norwood, NJ: Ablex.

Marzano, R. J. (2003). *What works in schools: Translating research into action.* Alexandria, VA: Association for Supervision and Curriculum Development.

Mattos, M., DuFour, R., DuFour, R., Eaker, R., & Many, T. W. (2016). *Concise answers to frequently asked questions about Professional Learning Communities at Work.* Bloomington, IN: Solution Tree Press.

McTighe, J., & Curtis, G. (2015). *Leading modern learning: A blueprint for vision-driven schools.* Bloomington, IN: Solution Tree Press.

McWilliam, E. L. (2009). Teaching for creativity: From sage to guide to meddler. *Asia Pacific Journal of Education, 29*(3). pp. 281–293.

Ministry of Education. (2007). *The New Zealand curriculum.* Wellington, New Zealand: Learning Media Limited.

National Council for the Social Studies. (2013). *The College, Career, and Civic Life (C3) framework for social studies state standards: Guidance for enhancing the rigor of K–12 civics, economics, geography, and history.* Silver Spring, MD: Author.

NuVu. (2018). *Hacking Wheelchairs for Urbanity.* Accessed at https://cambridge .nuvustudio.com/studios/hacking-a-wheelchair#tab-feed-url on January 5, 2018.

Partnership for 21st Century Learning. (2016). *Framework for 21st century learning.* Accessed at www.p21.org/our-work/p21-framework on October 12, 2017.

Perkins, D. N. (2014). *Future wise: Educating our children for a changing world.* San Francisco: Jossey-Bass.

Reeves, D. (2005). Putting it all together: Standards, assessment, and accountability in successful professional learning communities. In R. DuFour, R. Eaker, & R. DuFour

(Eds.), *On common ground: The power of professional learning communities* (pp. 45–63). Bloomington, IN: Solution Tree Press.

Ritchhart, R., Church, M., & Morrison, K. (2011). *Making thinking visible: How to promote engagement, understanding, and independence for all learners.* San Francisco: Jossey-Bass.

Schmoker, M. (2005). No turning back: The ironclad case for professional learning communities. In R. DuFour, R. Eaker, & R. DuFour (Eds.), *On common ground: The power of professional learning communities* (pp. 135–154). Bloomington, IN: Solution Tree Press.

Vander Ark, T. (2016, May 31). *Visiting schools: Transformative professional learning.* Accessed at www.gettingsmart.com/2016/05/transformative-professional-learning/201 on October 12, 2017.

Urban, W., & Wagoner, J. (2013). *American education: A history.* New York: Routledge.

Wagner, T. (2008). *The global achievement gap: Why even our best schools don't teach the new survival skills our children need and what we can do about it.* New York: Basic Books.

Wagner, T. (2012). *Creating innovators: The making of young people who will change the world.* New York: Scribner.

Wagner, T., & Dintersmith, T. (2016). *Most likely to succeed: Preparing our kids for the innovation era* [Kindle version]. New York: Scribner.

Wiggins, G., & McTighe, J. (2007). *Schooling by design: Mission, action, and achievement.* Alexandria, VA: Association for Supervision and Curriculum Development.

# Index

## Learning by Doing
### *Richard DuFour, Rebecca DuFour, Robert Eaker, and Thomas W. Many*

This book is an action guide for closing the knowing-doing gap and transforming schools into PLCs. It includes seven major additions that equip educators with essential tools for confronting challenges.

**BKF416**

## Taking Action: A Handbook for RTI at Work™
### *Austin Buffum, Mike Mattos, and Janet Malone*

This comprehensive implementation guide covers every element required to build a successful RTI at Work™ program in schools. The authors share step-by-step actions for implementing the essential elements, the tools needed to support implementation, and tips for engaging and supporting educators.

**BKF684**

## Simplifying Response to Intervention
### *Austin Buffum, Mike Mattos, and Chris Weber*

The follow-up to Pyramid Response to Intervention advocates that effective RTI begins by asking the right questions to create a fundamentally effective learning environment for every student. Understand why paperwork-heavy, compliance-oriented, test-score-driven approaches fail. Then learn how to create an RTI model that works.

**BKF506**

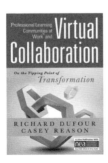

## Creating a Coaching Culture for Professional Learning Communities
### *Jane A. G. Kise and Beth Russell*

This practical resource provides activities designed to meet a wide variety of needs so you can choose the ones that fit your leadership style, the learning styles of team members, and the particular needs of the school.

**BKF350**

# "Tremendous, tremendous, tremendous!

The speaker made me do some very deep internal reflection about the **PLC process** and the personal responsibility I have in making the school improvement process work **for ALL kids."**

—Marc Rodriguez, teacher effectiveness coach,
Denver Public Schools, Colorado

## PD Services

Our experts draw from decades of research and their own experiences to bring you practical strategies for building and sustaining a high-performing PLC. You can choose from a range of customizable services, from a one-day overview to a multiyear process.

### Book your PLC PD today!
888.763.9045

Solution Tree